Wings of Joy

BY Joan Winmill Brown
No Longer Alone
Wings of Joy

Wings of Joy

compiled and edited by

Joan Winmill Brown

Fleming H. Revell Company
Old Tappan, New Jersey

Scripture quotations in this volume are from the King James Version of the Bible, unless otherwise identified.

The Scripture quotation identified MOFFATT is from THE BIBLE: A NEW TRANSLATION by James Moffatt. Copyright 1954 by James A. R. Moffatt. By permission of Harper & Row, Publishers, Inc.

ISBN 0-8007-0877-6

Copyright © 1977 by Joan Winmill Brown
Published by Fleming H. Revell Company
All rights reserved
Library of Congress Catalog Card Number: 77-88800
Printed in the United States of America

Acknowledgments

Acknowledgment is made to the following for permission to reprint copyrighted material:

A & C BLACK LIMITED: Excerpt from *Philosophy of Civilization* by Albert Schweitzer is used by permission of A & C Black Limited, the publishers.

ABINGDON PRESS: "The Secret" is from *Spiritual Hilltops* by Ralph S. Cushman. Abingdon Press; excerpts by Ramsay MacDonald, Wilfred Grenfell, Madame Chiang Kai-shek, E. Stanley Jones, H. G. Wells, Theodore Roosevelt, and Samuel Ullman are from A TREASURY OF SERMON ILLUSTRATIONS edited by Charles Wallis.

ASSOCIATED PRESS: "I Thank the Lord" by Ralph Gaither is reprinted by permission of the Associated Press.

BILLY GRAHAM EVANGELISTIC ASSOCIATION: Excerpt from DECISION by Sherwood E. Wirt © 1973 by the Billy Graham Evangelistic Association; excerpt from DECISION by Ricks L. Falk © 1976 by the Billy Graham Evangelistic Association; excerpt by Bonnie Barrows Thomas is from DECISION © 1976 by the Billy Graham Evangelistic Association; excerpt from DAY BY DAY WITH BILLY GRAHAM compiled by Joan Winmill Brown © 1976 by the Billy Graham Evangelistic Association; excerpt from OUR CHRISTMAS STORY by Mrs. Billy Graham © 1959 by the Billy Graham Evangelistic Association. Used by permission.

CHOSEN BOOKS, INC.: Excerpt from *Adventures in Prayer*. Copyright © 1975 by Catherine Marshall. Published by Chosen Books, Inc.; excerpts from THE HIDING PLACE © 1971 by Corrie ten Boom and John and Elizabeth Sherrill. Published by Chosen Books, Inc.

CHRISTIAN LITERATURE CRUSADE: Excerpt by Norman Grubb from *Rees Howells Intercessor* (Guildford: Lutterworth Press, 1952, and Fort Washington: Christian Literature Crusade, Inc.). Used by permission.

CONCERN, INC.: Excerpt by Dr. Richard C. Halverson is from *Perspective*, a bi-weekly devotional letter published by Concern, Inc., Washington, D.C.

PETER DAVIES LTD.: Excerpts from "The Verdict of the Empty Tomb," and "Were You There?" are from MR. JONES, MEET THE MASTER (British edition) by Peter Marshall and are used by permission of Catherine Marshall.

DOUBLEDAY & CO., INC.: "If" copyright 1910 by Rudyard Kipling from RUDYARD KIPLING'S VERSE: DEFINITIVE EDITION; "For A Friend" originally titled "For A Friend As Prayer For A Friend" copyright © 1968 by The Evening Star Newspaper from I'VE GOT TO TALK TO SOMEBODY, GOD by Marjorie Holmes. Reprinted by permission of Doubleday & Company, Inc.; excerpt from HIS EYE IS ON THE SPARROW by Ethel Waters. Copyright 1950, 1951, by Ethel Waters and Charles Samuels; excerpt from ANGELS—GOD'S SECRET AGENTS by Billy Graham. Copyright © 1975 by Billy Graham. Excerpt from PEACE WITH GOD by Billy Graham. Copyright 1953; excerpt from THE STORY OF MY LIFE by Helen Keller. Reprinted by permission of Doubleday & Company, Inc.

FIELD NEWSPAPER SYNDICATE: The Ann Landers column is reprinted from the Los Angeles *Herald-Examiner* by permission of Miss Landers and the Field Newspaper Syndicate.

GOSPEL LIGHT PUBLICATIONS: Reprinted from IF I SHOULD WAKE BEFORE I DIE by Lloyd John Ogilvie. © Copyright 1974 by Gospel Light Publications, Glendale, CA 91209. Used by permission.

HARPER & ROW PUBLISHERS: Excerpt from THE WEB AND THE ROCK by Thomas Wolfe; excerpt from TO ME IT'S WONDERFUL by Ethel Waters. Copyright © 1972 by Ethel Waters; from POEMS OF INSPIRATION AND COURAGE (1965) by Grace Noll Crowell: "Let Us Keep Christmas," copyright, 1950 by Harper & Row, Publishers, Inc.; "So Long as There Are Homes"—Copyright 1936 by Harper & Row, Publishers, Inc.; from SONGS OF HOPE by Grace Noll Crowell: "To One in Sorrow," copyright 1938 by Harper & Row, Publishers, Inc.; "I Have Found Such Joy" in LIGHT OF THE YEARS by Grace Noll Crowell. Copyright 1936 by Harper & Row, Publishers, Inc.; excerpt from THIS I REMEMBER by Eleanor Roosevelt, Harper & Row, 1949; excerpt from SOMETHING BEAUTIFUL FOR GOD: Mother Teresa of Calcutta. Malcolm Muggeridge, Harper & Row, 1971; excerpt from PROFILES IN COURAGE by John F. Kennedy; selected excerpts by Norman Vincent Peale and Joseph R. Sizoo are from WORDS OF LIFE; selected excerpts by Sir Cecil Spring-Rice and Joseph Johnston Lee are from MASTERPIECES OF RELIGIOUS VERSE; selected excerpts by Henry Van Dyke, E. Stanley Jones, Adlai Stevenson, Franklin D. Roosevelt, Dwight D. Eisenhower, G. K. Chesterton, Albert Einstein, L. Nelson Bell, Albert Schweitzer and Anne Campbell are from *The Treasure Chest*. Reprinted by permission of Harper & Row, Publishers.

HAWTHORNE BOOKS, INC.: Reprinted by permission of Hawthorne Books, Inc., excerpt from THREE TO GET MARRIED by Fulton J. Sheen. Copyright © 1951, by Fulton J. Sheen. All rights reserved.

HODDER & STOUGHTON LTD.: "Faith" by G. A. Studdert-Kennedy is from THE UNUTTERABLE BEAUTY; "Peace and Joy" by G. A. Studdert-Kennedy is from THE BEST OF STUDDERT-KENNEDY. Used by permission of Hodder & Stoughton Limited, Publishers.

HOUSE OF CASH: "I Prayed for Greater Joy" by Johnny Cash is used by permission of the publisher "House of Cash."

I.H.T.: "High Flight" by John Gillespie Magee, Jr., is originally from the New York *Herald Tribune*, used by permission of I.H.T. Corporation.

ALFRED A. KNOPF, INC.: Excerpt from "The Children" reprinted from THE PROPHET, by Kahlil Gibran, with permission of the publisher, Alfred A. Knopf, Inc. Copyright 1923 by Kahlil Gibran; renewal copyright 1951 by Administrators C.T.A. of Kahlil Gibran Estate, and Mary G. Gibran.

5

J. B. LIPPINCOTT COMPANY: "Harbour Lights" is from COL-LECTED POEMS In One Volume by Alfred Noyes. Copyright 1906, renewed 1934 by Alfred Noyes. Reprinted by permission of J. B. Lippincott Company.

LITTLE, BROWN AND COMPANY: Poetry by Emily Dickinson is from ' JEMS, edited by Martha Dickinson Bianchi and Alfred Leete Hampson, published by Little, Brown and Company.

MACMILLAN PUBLISHING COMPANY: Reprinted with permission of Macmillan Publishing Co., Inc., from LETTERS AND PAPERS FROM PRISON, Rev. Edn., "Prayer for His Fellow Prisoners" by Dietrich Bonhoeffer. © SCM Press, Ltd. 1967. Copyright 1953 by Macmillan Publishing Co., Inc.; reprinted with permission of Macmillan Publishing Co., Inc.; from POEMS by John Masefield: "The Everlasting Mercy." Copyright 1912 by Macmillan Publishing Co., Inc., renewed 1940 by John Masefield.

MC GRAW-HILL BOOK COMPANY: Excerpt from A MAN CALLED PETER by Catherine Marshall. Copyright, 1951. McGraw-Hill Book Co.; excerpt from REMINISCENCES, by General of the Army Douglas MacArthur, McGraw-Hill Book Co., © 1964 Time Inc. All rights reserved; excerpts from THE PRAYERS OF PETER MARSHALL by Catherine Marshall are used by permission of the McGraw-Hill Book Company.

WILLIAM MORROW & COMPANY: "Sixteen" by Viola Downen is reprinted by permission of William Morrow & Company, Inc. from TED MALONE'S SCRAPBOOK. Copyright © 1941 by William Morrow & Company.

OVERSEAS MISSIONARY FELLOWSHIP: Excerpt from THE TRIUMPH OF JOHN AND BETTY STAM by Mrs. Howard Taylor is reprinted courtesy of Overseas Missionary Fellowship.

JOHN OXENHAM's poetry is used by permission of T. Oxenham.

OXFORD UNIVERSITY PRESS: Poem by Robert Bridges is from The Poetical Works of Robert Bridges, published by Oxford University Press. Reprinted by permission of the publisher.

FLEMING H. REVELL COMPANY: Excerpt by Marabel Morgan is from TOTAL JOY. Copyright © 1976 by Marabel Morgan. Published by Fleming H. Revell Company; excerpt by Joyce Landorf is from MOURNING SONG. Copyright © 1974 by Fleming H. Revell Company; excerpts from THE WOMAN AT THE WELL by Dale Evans Rogers. Copyright © 1970 by Fleming H. Revell Company; excerpt from LOVE IS AN EVERYDAY THING by Colleen Townsend Evans. Copyright © 1974 by Fleming H. Revell Company; "Hold My Hand" and "Communion" are from AFTER THE RAIN by Ione W. Lyall. Copyright © 1975 by Fleming H. Revell Company; excerpt by Robert H. Schuller is from THE GREATEST POSSIBILITY THINKER THAT EVER LIVED.

Copyright © 1973 by Fleming H. Revell Company; excerpts from the writings of Charles L. Allen are used by permission of Fleming H. Revell Company; excerpt by Anita Bryant is from BLESS THIS HOUSE. Copyright © 1972 by Fleming H. Revell Company; excerpt by Dr. James Dobson is from HIDE OR SEEK. Copyright © 1974 by Fleming H. Revell Company; excerpt by Sherwood E. Wirt is from The Quiet Corner (A devotional treasury from the pages of Decision magazine), edited by Sherwood Wirt. Copyright © 1965 by Sherwood Wirt. Published by Fleming H. Revell Company. Unless otherwise identified, excerpts by Peter Marshall are from Mr. Jones, Meet the Master. Copyright © 1949, 1950 by Fleming H. Revell Company.

CHARLES SCRIBNER'S SONS: The following poems by Henry Van Dyke are reprinted with the permission of Charles Scribner's Sons: "The Voyagers" from SIX DAYS OF THE WEEK (copyright 1924 Charles Scribner's Sons) "These Are the Things I Prize" from MUSIC AND OTHER POEMS; excerpts reprinted from THE DIARY OF PRIVATE PRAYER by John Baillie with the permission of Charles Scribner's Sons. Copyright 1949 Charles Scribner's Sons.

SHEED & WARD, INC.: Excerpt from THE COMPLETE WORKS OF ST. TERESA translated and edited by E. Allison Peers from the critical edition of P. Silvero de Santa Teresa, C.D., published in three volumes by Sheed and Ward, Inc., New York.

THE SOCIETY OF AUTHORS: Excerpts from the writings of Bernard Shaw used by permission of The Society of Authors on behalf of the Bernard Shaw estate.

SPCK: Excerpt from "The Last Defile" by Amy Carmichael is from Amy Carmichael of Dohnavur by Frank Houghton, London SPCK; poem from Toward Jerusalem by Amy Carmichael is used by permission of London SPCK.

TYNDALE HOUSE PUBLISHERS: Excerpt from Lane Adams is from his book How Come It's Taking Me So Long to Get Better? published by Tyndale House; excerpt from Norma by Norma Zimmer copyright © 1976 by Tyndale House Publishers, Wheaton, Illinois. Used by permission.

ZONDERVAN PUBLISHING HOUSE: Excerpts from A SHEPHERD LOOKS AT PSALM 23 by W. Phillip Keller. Copyright © 1970 by W. Phillip Keller. Used by permission; excerpt from HIS STUBBORN LOVE by Joyce Landorf. Copyright © 1971 by Zondervan Publishing House. Used by permission.

The author is indebted to BELOVED YANKEE by David Wimbey for information on David Brainerd, and to MARRIAGE TO A DIFFICULT MAN by Elizabeth D. Dodds for information about the Jonathan Edwards family.

Contents

Introduction

Let us be like a bird for a moment perched
On a frail branch while he sings;
Though he feels it bend, yet he sings his song,
Knowing that he has wings.
                                        —VICTOR HUGO

There havé been many times in my life when I have felt the branch beneath me "bend"—seemingly to send me crashing downwards—but I am so thankful that "wings of joy" have enabled me to soar upwards. These "wings" have come from the Scriptures, from poetry (often written hundreds of years ago), or from a piece of prose.

Sir James Barrie once said, "To have faith is to have wings." As you read this book, you will encounter the faith of people like Corrie ten Boom, who experienced the tremendous comfort of God's love in the darkest of all places, a concentration camp; Peter Marshall, who became Chaplain of the United States Senate and whose infectious love for Christ still reaches out from the written word; the mother of John Newton, who prayed for her son—the son who later turned from being a slave trader to become a man who inspired hundreds by his preaching, and still goes on inspiring with his universally loved hymn "Amazing Grace." You will meet, too, a woman who was Queen of England, yet realized that her high station in life did not protect her from the tragedies that everyone faces. As you read these stories and many more, the overwhelmingly tremendous truth comes leaping from the pages that God does love each one of us and is always ready to hear our prayers and comfort us.

These inspiring "wings of joy" have become mine, and my prayer is that they will become yours too. Also, that this book will not just be put on a shelf, but will really become a "friend" that you will reach out to in all the circumstances of your life.

I have collected these thoughts of others, who have inspired the world, with the hope that in reading them we may realize that whatever happens to us in life—the joys, the tragedies, the everyday trials—these have all been experienced by others to some degree. Our deep feelings are not unique, but have been encountered down through the centuries. It is with this in mind I have sought to compile these masterpieces of literature (along with the "lighter" things that I have included). Some, you will find familiar, others new. Each day I seem to find somewhere a new "wing" on which to soar and this has presented a problem in making this compilation—where to stop!

Always an avid reader, I found it difficult to find time for any lengthy reading when my children were small; actually it was impossible. We moved from city to city in my husband's work (my older son had twenty-two homes by the time he was fourteen), so only a few books could be taken with me. For example, I had been given a small book of Elizabeth Barrett Browning's sonnets and the stories behind them. Over and over again I would refer to those incredibly beautiful words—escaping for a moment the world of Pampers, Pablum, and pandemonium!

These "wings of joy" have been gathered over the years and I still go on collecting them. I share them with you now that they might become a part of that wonderful world we can all have—a private inspirational library we can refer to constantly.

When I was a small child I can remember that my greatest pleasure was to be taken to London by my father and my favorite place to visit was Buckingham Palace. As we drew near I always hoped that the royal flag was flying—this meant that the king was in residence. It always gave me great joy to think that even if I could not see him, he was there with the royal family. Later on in my life I was to encounter Jesus Christ, the King of kings, who came to live in my heart. Someone once described it so beautifully:

> Joy is the masthead that flys over the palace
> of the heart when the King is in residence.

May *Wings of Joy* bring you Christ's love and comfort, knowing that He wants to live in all our hearts, if only we are willing to let Him.

I want to thank the publishers for giving me the absolute delight of being able to bring this book together. It gave me a wonderful excuse to read and read and read, even when there was absolute chaos in the house. "But I'm working!" I could honestly say, when my family wanted to know why nothing had been done amid all the confusion. To my husband, Bill, who tirelessly kept me from completely becoming a bookworm and got me actively piecing all the "treasure" together, and to June Self, whose typing brought order out of all my complicated notes—many, many thank-yous.

—J. W. B.

JOAN WINMILL BROWN

Wings of Joy

The greatest happiness of life is the conviction
that we are loved, loved for ourselves, or rather
in spite of ourselves.

—VICTOR HUGO

As we read literature from out of the past, there is always evident the longing
to be loved. What miracles happen when someone *is* loved! From the
standpoint of *human love,* perhaps nowhere can we find a better example than
in the case of Elizabeth Barrett Browning.

Before she met Robert Browning, Elizabeth was confined to her room, always
facing the hardship of ill health and a father who forbade any of his eleven
children to marry or have any visitors. When she first received a letter from
Browning, her small world was suddenly opened up and she began to live with
hope and anticipation.

"I love your verses with all my heart, dear Miss Barrett . . . and I love you,
too." These words broke through the stifling loneliness and brought to
Elizabeth belief that life was not finished for her, but just beginning.

She quickly returned Robert Browning's love, and after marrying him secretly, she escaped the "prison" of her father's house and went to Italy. There
the couple lived for fifteen happy years. Elizabeth's health improved and she
gave birth to a son. When she died in the arms of her husband, her last word
was *beautiful.*

The love sonnets that were published under the title *Sonnets from the Portuguese* ("Portuguese" being Robert Browning's nickname for his beloved
brunette wife) were indeed beautiful. The Brownings' favorite became the
world's favorite and has been described as the best-loved poem of lovers down
through the years. Written by Elizabeth, it reads:

How do I love thee? Let me count the ways.
I love thee to the depth and breadth and height
My soul can reach, when feeling out of sight

For the ends of Being and ideal Grace.
I love thee to the level of every day's
Most quiet need, by sun and candlelight.
I love thee freely, as men strive for Right;
I love thee purely, as they turn from Praise.
I love thee with the passion put to use
In my old griefs, and with my childhood's faith.
I love thee with a love I seemed to lose
With my lost saints—I love thee with the breath,
Smiles, tears, of all my life!—and, if God choose,
I shall but love thee better after death.

The eternal search of mankind always is to love and to be loved. The ultimate
of love, however, is to know God's *divine love* in our lives—to feel that no matter
how far we have failed, we are loved not for our achievements, but for ourselves. These words by Dr. Richard C. Halverson ring with the assurance of
God's unchanging love:

> There is nothing you can do . . .
> *To make God love you more!*
>
> There is nothing you can do . . .
> *To make God love you less!*
>
> His love is . . .
> *Unconditional . . .*
> *Impartial . . .*
> *Everlasting . . .*
> *Infinite . . .*
> *Perfect!*
> God is love!

> God commendeth his love toward us, in
> that, while we were yet sinners, Christ
> died for us.
>
> Romans 5:8
>
> —*J. W. B.*

> He loves each one of us, as if there were
> only one of us.
>
> SAINT AUGUSTINE

We sometimes fear to bring our troubles to
God, because they must seem so small to
Him who sitteth on the circle of the earth.
But if they are large enough to vex and en-
danger our welfare, they are large enough
to touch His heart of love. For love does not
measure by a merchant's scales, nor with a
surveyor's chain. It hath a delicacy which is
unknown in any handling of material sub-
stances.

                                    R. A. TORREY

There are many who want me to tell them
of secret ways of becoming perfect and I
can only tell them that the sole secret is a
hearty love of God, and the only way of
attaining that love is by loving. You learn
to speak by speaking, to study by study-
ing, to run by running, to work by working; and just so you learn to love God and
man by loving. Begin as a mere apprentice
and the very power of love will lead you on
to become a master of the art.

                              FRANCIS DE SALES

I love, my God, but with no love of mine,
    For I have none to give;
I love Thee, Lord, but all the love is Thine,
    For by Thy life I live.
I am as nothing, and rejoice to be
Emptied and lost and swallowed up in Thee.

Thou, Lord, alone art all Thy children need,
    And there is none beside;
From Thee the streams of blessedness proceed;
    In Thee the blest abide,
Fountain of life, and all-abounding grace,
Our source, our center, and our dwelling-place!

            MADAME JEANNE MARIE GUYON

Father, let me hold thy hand and like a
child walk with Thee down all my days,
secure in thy love and strength.

THOMAS À KEMPIS

There is an ocean—cold water without mo-
tion. In this ocean, however, is the Gulf
Stream, hot water flowing from the equator
toward the Pole. Inquire of all scientists
how it is physically imaginable that a
stream of hot water flows between the waters of the ocean, which, so to speak, form
its banks, the moving within the motion-
less, the hot within the cold. No scientist
can explain it. Similarly, there is the God of
love within the God of the forces of the
universe—one with Him, and yet so totally
different. We let ourselves be seized and
carried away by that vital stream.

ALBERT SCHWEITZER

WHAT MORE CAN YOU ASK

God's love endureth forever—
What a wonderful thing to know
When the tides of life run against you
And your spirit is downcast and low . . .
God's kindness is ever around you,
Always ready to freely impart
Strength to your faltering spirit,
Cheer to your lonely heart . . .
God's presence is ever beside you,
As near as the reach of your hand,
You have but to tell Him your troubles,
There is nothing He won't understand . . .
And knowing God's love is unfailing,
And His mercy unending and great,
You have but to trust in His promise—
"God comes not too soon or too late" . . .
So wait with a heart that is patient

For the goodness of God to prevail—
For never do prayers go unanswered,
And His mercy and love never fail.

HELEN STEINER RICE

Eye hath not seen, nor ear heard, neither
have entered into the heart of man, the
things which God hath prepared for them
that love him.

1 Corinthians 2:9

When I come to the Lord's Table and partake of the communion service which is a feast of thanksgiving for His love and care, do I fully appreciate what it has cost Him to prepare this table for me?

Here we commemorate the greatest and deepest demonstration of *true love* the world has ever known. For God looked down upon sorrowing, struggling, sinning humanity and was moved with compassion for the contrary, sheep-like creatures He had made. In spite of the tremendous personal cost it would entail to Himself to deliver them from their dilemma He chose deliberately to descend and live amongst them that He might deliver them.

This meant laying aside His splendor, His position, His prerogatives as the perfect and faultless One. He knew He would be exposed to terrible privation, to ridicule, to false accusations, to rumor, gossip and malicious charges that branded Him as a glutton, drunkard, friend of sinners and even an imposter. It entailed losing His reputation. It would involve physical suffering, mental anguish and spiritual agony.

In short, His coming to earth as the Christ, as Jesus of Nazareth, was a straightforward case of utter self-sacrifice that culminated in the cross of Calvary. The laid-down life, the poured-out blood were the supreme symbols of total selflessness. This was *love*. This was *God*. This was *divinity* in action, delivering men from their own utter selfishness, their own stupidity, their own suicidal instincts as lost sheep unable to help themselves.

W. PHILLIP KELLER
A Shepherd Looks at Psalm 23

I thank the Lord for blessings big and small;
For spring's warm glow and songbird's welcome call;
For autumn's hue and winter's snow white shawl.

I thank Thee for each sunset in the sky;
For sleepy nights, the bed in which I lie;
A life of truth and peace, a woman's love;
Her hand in mine until the day I die.
I thank Thee Lord, for all these things above;
But most of all, I thank Thee for Thy love.
    Written by COMMANDER RALPH GAITHER
    while a prisoner for seven and a half years in
    a North Vietnamese prison camp.

God's love still stands when all else has fallen. First Corinthians 13:

In my life everything had fallen. I stood on roll call in a concentration camp where 96,000 women died or were killed. In front of me stood a guard who used his time to demonstrate his cruelties. I could hardly bear to see and hear what happened in front of us. Suddenly a skylark started to sing in the sky. All the prisoners looked up and listened to the bird's song. When I looked at the bird I looked further at the sky and I remembered Psalm 103.

"As the heaven is high above the earth, so great is God's mercy and love toward them that fear Him."

It was as if I woke up to reality! I saw that God's love still stood. O love of God, how deep and great. Far deeper than man's deepest hate.

God sent that skylark daily for three weeks, exactly during roll call time to keep my eyes turned in the right direction.

CORRIE TEN BOOM
The Hiding Place

Beloved, let us love one another: for love
is of God; and every one that loveth is born
of God, and knoweth God.
   . . . If we love one another, God dwelleth in us, and his love is perfected in us.
   . . . God is love; and he that dwelleth in
love dwelleth in God, and God in him.
   And this commandment have we from
him, That he who loveth God love his
brother also.
1 John 4:7, 12, 16, 21

If I had only one day to see people for what they really are, I would want to look beyond all the things that are so obvious to my eyes . . . all the imperfections and even the glaring mistakes in their lives. I would want to look at the inner person, not at the outer garments . . . I hope I would get down to basics and look for the good in each man and woman, because that's what really counts. I hope I would see each one as God sees him . . . for though we may say *no* to God—God never rejects anyone. I guess what I'm really saying is that I hope I would *hope*—because that's the best way I can say, "I love you."

COLLEEN TOWNSEND EVANS
Love Is an Everyday Thing

We shall never agree on every issue but we can admit that the other fellow has a right to his opinions, and even though we differ, we do not need to hate. We are all human. As Alexander Pope said, "To err is human; to forgive, divine." Disagreements can and often do turn into hatreds; they breed fights and fatal dissensions in the Church, and I hate *that*. What would happen if every marriage broke up over every disagreement of man and wife? What would happen to the children then? And what happens to the babes in Christ when older, more experienced Christians fall out in quarrel and disagreement? What's a babe to do—and what and whom is he to believe?

Again, love is the answer—godly, unselfish love for one's neighbor. Love is of no one color; it's made up of all colors. Since we were all created in His image and in His love, can we do less than love all His creatures?

DALE EVANS ROGERS
The Woman at the Well

A new commandment I give unto you, That ye love one another; as I have loved you, that ye also love one another.

John 13:34

Never let the seeming worthlessness of sympathy make you keep back that sympathy of which, when men are suffering around you, your heart is full. Go and give it without asking yourself whether it is

worthwhile to give it. It is too sacred a
thing for you to tell what it is worth. God,
from whom it comes, sends it through you
to His needy child.

PHILLIPS BROOKS

That best portion of a good man's life,—
His little nameless, unremembered acts
Of kindness and of love.

WILLIAM WORDSWORTH

You who are letting miserable misunderstandings run on from year to
year, meaning to clear them up some day;

You who are keeping wretched quarrels alive because you cannot
quite make up your mind that now is the day to sacrifice your pride and
kill them;

You who are passing men sullenly upon the street, not speaking to
them out of some silly spite, and yet knowing that it would fill you with
shame and remorse if you heard that one of those men were dead tomorrow morning;

You who are letting your neighbor starve, till you hear that he is dying
of starvation;

Or letting your friend's heart ache for a word of appreciation or sympathy, which you mean to give him someday;

If you only could know and see and feel, all of a sudden, that *"the time
is short,"* how it would break the spell! How you would go instantly and
do the thing which you might never have another chance to do.

PHILLIPS BROOKS

Strive to love your neighbor actively and indefatigably. In as far as
you advance in love you will grow surer of the reality of God and of the
immortality of your soul. If you attain to perfect self-forgetfulness in the
love of your neighbor, then you will believe without doubt, and no
doubt can possibly enter your soul . . . .

FËDOR DOSTOEVSKI
The Brothers Karamazov

. . . thou shalt love thy neighbour as thyself . . . .

Leviticus 19:18

I sought my soul,
 But my soul I could not see.
I sought my God,
 But my God eluded me.
I sought my brother,
 And I found all three.

AUTHOR UNKNOWN

We never live so intensely as when we love
 strongly.
We never realize ourselves so vividly as
 when we are in the full glow of love for
 others.

WALTER RAUSCHENBUSCH

GERMAN PRISONERS

When first I saw you in the curious street
Like some platoon of soldier ghosts in grey,
My mad impulse was all to smite and slay,
To spit upon you—tread you 'neath my feet.
But when I saw how each sad soul did greet
My gaze with no sign of defiant frown,
How from tired eyes looked spirits broken down,
How each face showed the pale flag of defeat,
And doubt, despair, and disillusionment,
And how were grievous wounds on many a head,
And on your garb red-faced was other red;
And how you stooped as men whose strength was spent,
I knew that we had suffered each as other,
And could have grasped your hand and cried, "My brother!"

JOSEPH JOHNSTON LEE
British Soldier

My soul is too glad and too great to be at
heart the enemy of any man.

MARTIN LUTHER

Ye have enemies; for who can live on this earth without them? Take
heed to yourselves: love them. In no way can thy enemy so hurt thee by
his violence as thou dost hurt thyself if thou love him not. And let it not

seem to you impossible to love him. Believe first that it can be done, and pray that the will of God may be done in you. For what good can thy neighbor's ill do to thee? If he had no ill, he would not even be thine enemy. Wish him well, then, that he may end his ill, and he will be thine enemy no longer. For it is not the human nature in him that is at enmity with thee, but his sin . . . Let thy prayer be against the malice of thine enemy, that it may die, and he may live. For if thine enemy were dead, thou hast lost, it might seem, an enemy, yet has thou not found a friend. But if his malice die, thou hast at once lost an enemy and found a friend.

SAINT AUGUSTINE

Those who love not their fellow beings live
unfruitful lives.

PERCY BYSSHE SHELLEY

To love one's neighbors, to love one's enemies, to love everything, to love God in all His manifestations. It is possible to love someone dear to you with human love, but an enemy can only be loved by divine love . . . .

"When loving with human love one may pass from love to hatred, but divine love cannot change. No, neither death nor anything else can destroy it. It is the very essence of the soul."

LEO TOLSTOY
War and Peace

Love has a hem to her garment
That trails in the very dust;
It can reach the stains of the streets and lanes,
And because it can, it *must*.

AUTHOR UNKNOWN

We like someone *because*. We love someone
although.

HENRI DE MONTHERLANT

As we have therefore opportunity, let us do
good unto all men . . . .

Galatians 6:10

He prayeth best, who loveth best
All things both great and small;
For the dear God who loveth us,
He made and loveth all.

SAMUEL T. COLERIDGE
The Rime of the Ancient Mariner

NO GREATER LOVE

In going or in giving,
In dying or in living,
I'll try to show the world it has a friend.
By praying and by caring,
By reaching out and sharing,
The love of Christ will go on without end, without end.

There is no greater love than this,
No greater love than this,
That a man should give his life to save another.
There is no greater love than this,
No greater love than this,
Make me willing Lord, at least to help my brother.

RALPH CARMICHAEL

Greater love hath no man than this, that a
man lay down his life for his friends.

John 15:13

Love is but the heart's immortal thirst
To be completely known and all forgiven.

HENRY VAN DYKE

Not father or mother has loved you as God
has, for it was that you might be happy He
gave His only Son. When He bowed His
head in the death hour, love solemnized its
triumph; the sacrifice there was completed.

HENRY WADSWORTH LONGFELLOW

All human beings have failings, all human beings have needs and temptations and stresses. Men and women who live together through long years get to know one another's failings; but they also come to know what is worthy of respect and admiration in those they live with and in themselves. If at the end one can say, "This man used to the limit the powers that God granted him; he was worthy of love and respect and of the sacrifices of many people, made in order that he might achieve what he deemed to be his task," then that life has been lived well and there are no regrets.

ELEANOR ROOSEVELT
This I Remember

If you would be loved, love and be lovable.
BENJAMIN FRANKLIN

For, lo, the winter is past, the rain is over
and gone; The flowers appear on the earth;
the time of the singing of birds is come,
and the voice of the turtle is heard in our
land; The fig tree putteth forth her green
figs, and the vines with the tender grape
give a good smell. Arise, my love, my fair
one, and come away.
Song of Solomon 2:11–13

I like not only to be loved, but to be told
that I am loved; the realm of silence is large
enough beyond the grave.
GEORGE ELIOT

Love is not blind—it sees more, not less.
But because it sees more, it is willing to see
less.
JULIUS GORDON

There is beauty in the forest
When the trees are green and fair,
There is beauty in the meadow
When wild flowers scent the air.
There is beauty in the sunlight

And the soft blue beams above.
Oh, the world is full of beauty
When the heart is full of love.

AUTHOR UNKNOWN

Love comforteth like sunshine after rain.

WILLIAM SHAKESPEARE
Venus and Adonis

Love looks through a telescope; envy, through a microscope.

HENRY W. SHAW

If music be the food of love, play on.
Give me excess of it, that, surfeiting,
The appetite may sicken, and so die.
That strain again! it had a dying fall:
O!, it came o'er my ear like the sweet sound
That breathes upon a bank of violets,
Stealing and giving odour! Enough!
        no more:
'Tis not so sweet now as it was before.

WILLIAM SHAKESPEARE
Twelfth Night

Love is never lost. If not reciprocated, it will flow back and soften and purify the heart.

WASHINGTON IRVING

Persons are to be loved; things are to be used.

REUEL HOWE

The most wonderful of all things in life, I believe, is the discovery of another human being with whom one's relationship has a glowing depth, beauty, and joy as the years increase. This inner progressiveness of love between two human beings is a most marvelous thing, it cannot be found by looking for it or by passionately wishing for it. It is a sort of Divine accident.

SIR HUGH WALPOLE

No cord or cable can draw so forcibly, or bind so fast, as love can do with a single thread.

ROBERT BURTON

Love is too young to know what conscience is;
Yet who knows not conscience is born of love?
Then, gentle cheater, urge not my amiss,
Lest guilty of my faults thy sweet self prove:
For, thou betraying me, I do betray
My nobler part to my gross body's treason;
My soul doth tell my body that he may
Triumph in love; flesh stays no further reason,
But rising at thy name doth point out thee
As his triumphant prize. Proud of this pride,
He is contented thy poor drudge to be,
To stand in thy affairs, fall by thy side.
   No want of conscience hold it that I call
   Her 'love' for whose dear love I rise and fall.

WILLIAM SHAKESPEARE
Sonnets

Love keeps the cold out better than a cloak.
It serves for food and raiment . . . .

HENRY WADSWORTH LONGFELLOW

A wise lover
values not so much
the gift of the lover
as the love of the giver.

THOMAS À KEMPIS

Of all the music that reached farthest into heaven, it is the beating of a loving heart.

HENRY WARD BEECHER

As boundless as the sea
My love as deep;
The more I give thee
The more I have,
For both are infinite.
WILLIAM SHAKESPEARE
Juliet from *Romeo and Juliet*

Love does not consist in gazing at each
other, but in looking outward together in
the same direction.
ANTOINE DE SAINT EXUPÉRY

Love cannot be forced, love cannot be
coaxed and teased. It comes out of Heaven,
unasked and unsought.
PEARL BUCK

Time flies,
Suns rise,
And shadows fall.
Let time go by.
Love is forever over all.
Sundial inscription

'Tis better to have loved and lost
Than never to have loved at all.
ALFRED TENNYSON

What we love we shall grow to resemble.
BERNARD OF CLAIRVAUX

Love is a good above all others, which
alone maketh every burden light.

Love is watchful, and whilst sleeping still
keeps watch; though fatigued is not weary;
though pressed is not forced.

Love is sincere, gentle, strong, patient,
faithful, prudent, long-suffering, manly.

Love is circumspect, humble, upright; not
weary, not fickle, nor intent on vain things;
sober, chaste, steadfast, quiet, and
guarded in all the senses.

THOMAS À KEMPIS

*Lord, this heart does not know how to love unselfishly. Fill it with
Your divine love, so that I can see each one I meet through Your
eyes. Thank You, Heavenly Father, for the love of Jesus Christ, in
whose name I pray. Amen.*

—J. W. B.

Comfort

Oh! there is never sorrow of heart
That shall lack a timely end,
If but to God we turn, and ask
Of Him to be our friend!
　　—WILLIAM WORDSWORTH

The picturesque, peaceful town of Haarlem in Holland, dominated by its magnificent church in the market square, was the scene of Corrie ten Boom's happy, well-regulated life. The warmth and love that exuded from the Beje, the family home and watch shop, were felt by everyone fortunate enough to know the ten Booms, all dedicated Christians.

Papa ten Boom would each day read the Bible to his family and pray with them—always telling of God's love and comfort. At night he climbed the stairs to say good-night to his children; his prayers assured them of God's care and presence. It was a time that Corrie especially looked forward to, but she recalled that there was one night that stands out in particular when she had been very frightened by an incident that had taken place during the day.

Her mother, always aware of any kindness she could do to help others less fortunate than herself, had heard of a poor woman whose baby had just died. Mama took Corrie and her sister Nollie to the poor young Mrs. Hoog to comfort her. As Corrie looked at the dead baby she was confronted for the first time with the reality of death. She had reached out and touched the little lifeless hand and it was cold! She tells about this in *The Hiding Place:*

> Still shivering with that cold, I followed
> Nollie up to our room and crept into bed
> beside her. At last we heard Father's
> footsteps winding up the stairs. It was the

31

best moment in every day, when he came up to tuck us in. We never fell asleep until he had arranged the blankets in his special way and laid his hand for a moment on each head. Then we tried not to move even a toe.

But that night as he stepped through the door I burst into tears. "I need you!" I sobbed. "You can't die! You can't!"

Beside me on the bed Nollie sat up. "We went to see Mrs. Hoog," she explained. "Corrie didn't eat her supper or anything."

Father sat down on the edge of the narrow bed. "Corrie," he began gently, "when you and I go to Amsterdam—when do I give you your ticket?"

I sniffed a few times, considering this.

"Why, just before we get on the train."

"Exactly. And our wise Father in heaven knows when we're going to need things, too. Don't run ahead of Him, Corrie. When the time comes that some of us will have to die, you will look into your heart and find the strength you need—just in time."

When war broke out in 1939 it was hard to believe that its horrendous tentacles would grip this quiet, loving family in its unmerciful grasp. Always taught to care for other people's needs, the sight of the persecution of the Jews by the Nazis led Corrie and her sister Betsie to shelter them in their home, with Papa ten Boom's permission. Each day they lived with the fact that they could be betrayed, and one night the dreaded knock of the Gestapo echoed through the house. Thrown into prison, separated from their beloved Papa, who was to die shortly afterwards, Corrie and Betsie learned of the comfort of the Lord even in the direst circumstances.

The horrors of Ravensbruck, a concentration camp for women in Germany, could not keep Christ's love and grace from these two women who loved Him. Each day they leaned completely on His strength, comforting others. In the freezing winter, gentle Betsie died from the harsh conditions of the camp, leaving Corrie desolate. But Corrie found that even in the deepest pit God is always there, and His comfort encompassed her.

—*J. W. B.*

I will lift up mine eyes unto the hills, from whence cometh my help.
My help cometh from the Lord, which made heaven and earth.
He will not suffer thy foot to be moved: he that keepeth thee will not
    slumber.
Behold, he that keepeth Israel shall neither slumber nor sleep.
The Lord is thy keeper: the Lord is thy shade upon thy right hand.
The sun shall not smite thee by day, nor the moon by night.
The Lord shall preserve thee from all evil: he shall preserve thy soul.
The Lord shall preserve thy going out and thy coming in from this time
    forth, and even for evermore.

Psalm 121

Be still, my soul: the Lord is on thy side;
Bear patiently the cross of grief or pain;
Leave to thy God to order and provide;
In every change He faithful will remain.
Be still, my soul; thy best, thy heavenly Friend
Through thorny ways leads to a joyful end.

KATHARINA VON SCHLEGEL

They that sow in tears shall reap in joy.

Psalms 126:5

CHRIST SPEAKS TO US
WHEN WE ARE FRIGHTENED

Pluck up thy courage, faint heart; what though thou be fearful, sorry
and weary, and standeth in great dread of most painful torments, be of
good comfort; for I myself, have vanquished the whole world, and yet
felt I far more fear, sorrow, weariness, and much more inward anguish
too, when I considered my most bitter, painful Passion to press so fast
upon me. He that is strong-hearted may find a thousand glorious valiant
martyrs whose ensample he may right joyously follow. But thou now, O
timorous and weak, silly sheep, think it sufficient for thee only to walk
after me, which am thy shepherd and governor, and so mistrust thyself
and put thy trust in me. Take hold on the hem of my garment, therefore;
from thence shalt thou perceive such strength and relief to proceed . . . .

SIR THOMAS MORE
Treatise on the Passion

TO ONE IN SORROW

Let me come in where you are weeping, friend,
And let me take your hand.
I, who have known a sorrow such as yours,
Can understand.
Let me come in—I would be very still
Beside you in your grief;
I would not bid you cease your weeping, friend,
Tears bring relief.
Let me come in—I would only breathe a prayer,
And hold your hand,
For I have known a sorrow such as yours,
And understand.

GRACE NOLL CROWELL

There is no grief which time does not
lessen and soften.

CICERO

And God shall wipe away all tears from
their eyes; and there shall be no more
death, neither sorrow, nor crying, neither
shall there be any more pain . . . .

Revelation 21:4

Thank You, Father, for these tears that have
carried me to the depth of Your love. How
could I have known Your fullness without
the emptiness, Your acceptance without
the rejection, Your forgiveness without my
failure, our togetherness without that
dreadful loneliness. You have brought me
to Gethsemane, and oh, the joy of finding
You already there! *Amen.*

BONNIE BARROWS THOMAS

I was a stricken deer, that left the herd
Long since; with many an arrow deep infixt
My panting side was charg'd, when I withdrew
To seek a tranquil death in distant shades.
There was I found by one who had himself
Been hurt by th' archers. In his side he bore,
And in his hands and feet, the cruel scars.
With gentle force soliciting the darts,
He drew them forth, and heal'd, and bade me live.
Since then, with few associates, in remote
And silent woods, I wander, far from those
My former partners of the peopled scene;
With few associates, and not wishing more.

WILLIAM COWPER
The Task (written while
suffering mental illness)

Without the shadow—nothing.
Sundial Inscription

Why art thou cast down, O my soul? and
why art thou disquieted within me? hope
thou in God . . . .

Psalms 42:5

The Lord watch between me and thee,
when we are absent one from another.

Genesis 31:49

God has many ways of drawing us to Himself. He sometimes hides
Himself from us; but *faith* alone, which will not fail us in time of need,
ought to be our support, and the foundation of our confidence, which
must be all in God.

I know not how God will dispose of me. I am always happy. All the
world suffer; and I, who deserve the severest discipline, feel joys so
continual and so great that I can scarce contain them.

I would willingly ask of God a part of your sufferings, but that I know
my weakness, which is so great that if He left me one moment to myself I
should be the most wretched man alive. And yet I know not how He can
leave me alone, because faith gives me as strong a conviction as sense

can do that He never forsakes us until we have first forsaken Him. Let us
fear to leave Him. Let us be always with Him. Let us live and die in His
presence. Do you pray for me as I for you? . . .

BROTHER LAWRENCE
The Practice of the Presence of God

He said not,
    "Thou shall not be tempested,
    Thou shall not be travailed,
    Thou shall not be afflicted,"
But he said,
    "Thou shall not be overcome."
MOTHER JULIAN OF NORWICH

SAINT TERESA'S BOOKMARK

Let nothing disturb thee;
Let nothing dismay thee;
All things pass:
God never changes.
Patience attains
All that it strives for.
He who has God
Finds he lacks nothing:
God alone suffices.
    Translated by E. ALLISON PEERS

Cast thy burden upon the Lord, and he
shall sustain thee . . . .
Psalms 55:22

CAST YOUR CARES ON GOD

Cast all your cares on God; that anchor holds.
Is He not yonder in those uttermost
Parts of the morning? If I flee to these,
Can I go from Him? And the sea is His,
The sea is His; He made it.

ALFRED TENNYSON
From *Enoch Arden*

Come unto me, all ye that labour and are
heavy laden, and I will give you rest.
> Matthew 11:28

IN THE HOUR OF MY DISTRESS

In the hour of my distress,
When temptations me oppress,
And when I my sins confess,
  Sweet Spirit comfort me!

When the house doth sigh and weep,
And the world is drowned in sleep,
Yet mine eyes the watch do keep;
  Sweet Spirit comfort me!

When (God knows) I'm tos't about,
Either with despair or doubt;
Yet before the glass be out,
  Sweet Spirit comfort me!

When the Judgment is revealed,
And that opened which was sealed,
When to Thee I have appealed;
  Sweet Spirit comfort me!
> ROBERT HERRICK

Don't think your case unique; it can be matched many times over.
Don't give yourself to pity; the temptation will be to feel sorry for yourself; a self-pitying self is a pitiable self; don't allow yourself to slip on
that. Don't give yourself to excessive grief. Many do it, thinking they
thereby show their love. Don't retail your sorrows; doing so will cause
them to grow. Don't resign yourself to sorrow and feel it will continue.
Don't complain; the more you complain about things the more things
you will have to complain about.
> E. STANLEY JONES

The soul would have no rainbow had the
eyes no tears.
> AUTHOR UNKNOWN

HOLD MY HAND

Lord, You understand!
    You heard the crash like sudden doom
    You saw the fear-dilated eyes
    of my soul survey the ground where lay
    the gloom-wrapped pieces of my hopes,
    shattered in less time than it could take
    a second hand to round the dial.

    Lord, You know the agony
    of a broken heart, and so,
    Dear Lord, please—hold my hand.

IONE LYALL

Just as there comes a warm sunbeam into
every cottage window, so comes a love-
beam of God's care and pity for every sepa-
rate need.

NATHANIEL HAWTHORNE

Christ does not leave us comfortless, but we have to be in dire
need of comfort to know the truth of His promise.

It is in times of calamity . . .
   in days and nights of sorrow and trouble
     that the presence
       the sufficiency
         and the sympathy of God grow very sure
           and very wonderful.

Then we find out that the grace of God is sufficient
for all our needs
   for every problem
    and for every difficulty
for every broken heart, and for every human sorrow.

It is in times of bereavement that one begins to understand the
meaning of immortality.

PETER MARSHALL
"The Problem of Falling Rocks"

The God who made our bodies is concerned about the needs of our bodies, and He is anxious for us to talk with Him about our physical needs.

Every morning the sun rises to warm the earth. If it were to fail to shine for just one minute, all life on the earth would die. The rains come to water the earth. There is fertility in the soil, life in the seeds, oxygen in the air. The providence of God is about us in unbelievable abundance every moment. But so often we just take it for granted.

With infinite love and compassion our Lord understood the human predicament. He had deep empathy with people; He saw their needs, their weaknesses, their desires, and their hurts. He understood and was concerned for people. Every word He spoke was uttered because He saw a need for that word in some human life. His concern was always to uplift and never to tear down, to heal and never hurt, to save and not condemn.

CHARLES L. ALLEN

SANCTUARY

'Mid all the traffic of the ways,
Turmoils without, within,
Make in my heart a quiet place,
And come and dwell therein:

A little shrine of quietness,
All sacred to Thyself,
Where Thou shalt all my soul possess,
And I may find myself:

A little shelter from life's stress,
Where I may lay me prone,
And bare my soul in lowliness
And know as I am known:

A little place of mystic grace,
Of self and sin swept bare,
Where I may look into Thy face,
And talk with Thee in prayer.

JOHN OXENHAM

ABIDE WITH ME

Abide with me—fast falls the eventide;
The darkness deepens: Lord, with me abide;
When other helpers fail, and comforts flee,
Help of the helpless, O abide with me.

I need thy presence every passing hour:
What but thy grace can foil the tempter's power?
Who like thyself my guide and stay can be?
Through cloud and sunshine, O abide with me.

HENRY FRANCIS LYTE

FOR ALL WHO NEED

For all who watch tonight—by land or sea or air—
O Father, may they know that Thou art with them there.

For all who weep tonight, the hearts that cannot rest,
Reveal Thy love, that wondrous love which gave for us Thy best.

For all who wake tonight, love's tender watch to keep,
Watcher Divine, Thyself draw nigh, Thou who dost never sleep.

For all who fear tonight, whate'er the dread may be,
We ask for them the perfect peace of hearts that rest in Thee.

Our own belov'd tonight, O Father, keep, and where
Our love and succor cannot reach, now bless them through our prayer.

And all who pray tonight, Thy wrestling hosts, O Lord,
Make weakness strong, let them prevail according to Thy word.

AUTHOR UNKNOWN

Hast thou not known? hast thou not heard, that the everlasting God, the Lord, the Creator of the ends of the earth, fainteth not, neither is weary? there is no searching of his understanding.

He giveth power to the faint; and to them that have no might he increaseth strength.

Even the youths shall faint and be weary, and the young men shall utterly fall:

But they that wait upon the Lord shall renew their strength; they shall mount up with wings as eagles; they shall run, and not be weary; they shall walk, and not faint.

Isaiah 40:28–31

UP-HILL

Does the road wind up-hill all the way?
Yes, to the very end.
Will the day's journey take the whole long day?
From morn to night, my friend.

But is there for the night a resting-place?
A roof for when the slow dark hours begin.
May not the darkness hide it from my face?
You cannot miss the inn.

Shall I find comfort, travel-sore and weak?
Of labor you shall find the sum.
Will there be beds for me and all who seek?
Yes, beds for all who come.

CHRISTINA G. ROSSETTI

Loving Father, Your comfort in time of sorrow enfolds me. When it seems everything is hopeless, I remember Your love and put my hand into Yours. Thank You for the strength You give, my Saviour and my Lord. Amen.

—*J. W. B.*

Prayer

Grant us grace, Almighty Father, so to pray as to deserve to be heard.

—JANE AUSTEN

Many years ago in a small, poverty-stricken house in London, there lived a hard-working woman. Her back was bent from years of standing day after day over a washtub, this being her only source of income. As she worked, she constantly prayed for her son who later was to run away to sea while only a teenager. She was aware that the Lord answers prayer and with this faith she never gave up hope that her son would one day give his life to Him. After she died her prayers were answered and her son, by then a slave trader, became the "sailor preacher" of London. John Newton brought thousands of men to Christ. His hymn "Amazing Grace," which has been sung by Christians all over the world, is today as meaningful as when he sat down and wrote the words—words which were his testimony of the grace and forgiveness of God.

John Newton's words reached a skeptical man of great learning named Thomas Scott, who had avowed he did not need a Saviour. Later Scott's writings led scores of people to the Lord, including William Cowper. Cowper's poetry and prose in turn touched so many, one being William Wilberforce, the British statesman who went on to work so vigilantly for the abolition of slavery.

The chain of influence goes on as people read and are inspired by the words of these men. Little did John Newton's mother dream that the prayers for her son would be used by the Lord to go on and on touching so many lives for Him!

—*J. W. B.*

What things soever ye desire, when ye pray, believe that ye receive them, and ye shall have them.

Mark 11:24

43

Why is prayer so startlingly effective when we admit our helplessness? First, as we have seen, because God insists upon our facing up to the true facts of our human situation. Thus we lay under our prayer-structure the firm foundation of truth rather than self-delusion or wishful thinking.

This recognition and acknowledgment of our helplessness is also the quickest way to that right attitude which God recognizes as essential to prayer. It deals a mortal blow to the most serious sin of all—man's independence that ignores God.

Another reason is that we cannot learn firsthand about God—what He is like, His love for us as individuals, and His real power—so long as we are relying on ourselves and other people. And fellowship with Jesus is the true purpose of life and the only foundation for eternity. It is real, this daily fellowship He offers us.

So if your every human plan and calculation has miscarried, if, one by one, human props have been knocked out, and doors have shut in your face, take heart. God is trying to get a message through to you, and the message is: "Stop depending on inadequate human resources. Let Me handle the matter."

CATHERINE MARSHALL
Adventures in Prayer

THE SECRET

I met God in the morning
  When my day was at its best,
And His presence came like sunrise,
  Like a glory in my breast.

All day long the Presence lingered,
  All day long He stayed with me,
And we sailed in perfect calmness
  O'er a very troubled sea.

Other ships were blown and battered,
  Other ships were sore distressed,
But the winds that seemed to drive them
  Brought to us a peace and rest.

Then I thought of other mornings,
  With a keen remorse of mind,
When I too had loosed the moorings,
  With the Presence left behind.

So I think I know the secret,
    Learned from many a troubled way:
    You must seek Him in the morning
    If you want Him through the day!
                  RALPH SPAULDING CUSHMAN
                  Spiritual Hilltops

The holy time is quiet . . .
Breathless with adoration . . .
The gentleness of heaven broods o'er the sea;
Listen! . . .
                  WILLIAM WORDSWORTH

How rare to find a soul still enough to hear
God speak.
                  FRANCQIS DE FÉNELON

He who runs from God in the morning will
scarcely find him the rest of the day.
                  JOHN BUNYAN

In 1913 Sir William Osler, one of the great physicians of his day, told the students at Yale University: "Begin the day with Christ and His prayer—you need no other. Creedless, with it you have religion: creed-stuffed, it will leaven any theological dough in which you stick. Learn to know your Bible . . . In forming character and in shaping conduct its touch has still its ancient power."

After this manner therefore pray ye: Our Father which art in heaven, Hallowed be thy name.
Thy kingdom come. Thy will be done in earth, as it is in heaven.
Give us this day our daily bread.
And forgive us our debts, as we forgive our debtors.
And lead us not into temptation, but deliver us from evil: For thine is the kingdom, and the power, and the glory, for ever. Amen.
                  Matthew 6:9–13

The Lord's Prayer contains the sum total of
religion and morals.
                  DUKE OF WELLINGTON

O God, grant us the serenity to accept
What cannot be changed;
The courage to change what can be changed;
And wisdom to know one from the other.

REINHOLD NIEBUHR

O God, early in the morning do I cry unto Thee.
Help me to pray, and to think only of Thee.
I cannot pray alone.
In me there is darkness,
But with Thee there is light.

I am lonely,
  but Thou leavest me not.
I am feeble in heart,
  but Thou leavest me not.
I am restless,
  but with Thee there is peace.
In me there is bitterness,
  but with Thee there is patience.
Thy ways are past understanding,
  but Thou knowest the way for me.

  Lord Jesus Christ,
Thou wast poor, and in misery,
  a captive and forsaken as I am.
Thou knowest all man's distress;
Thou abidest with me when all others have deserted me;
Thou wilt not forget me, Thou seekest me.
Thou willest that I should know Thee and turn to Thee.
Lord, I hear Thy call and follow Thee;
  do Thou help me . . . .

I would remember before Thee
  all my loved ones,
  my fellow prisoners,
  and all who in this house perform their hard service.
  Lord have mercy.
Restore my liberty and enable me so to live that I may
  answer before Thee and before the world.

Lord, whatsoever this day may bring,
   Thy name be praised.
Be gracious unto me and help me.
Grant me strength to bear whatsoever Thou dost send,
And let not fear overrule me.
I trust Thy grace, and commit my life wholly into Thy
    Hands.
Whether I live or whether I die, I am with Thee,
And Thou art with me,
                 O my Lord and my God.
Lord, I wait for Thy salvation,
   and for the coming of Thy Kingdom. *Amen.*

> DIETRICH BONHOEFFER (*Letters and Papers
> from Prison*), written Christmas, 1943,
> while awaiting execution in a concen-
> tration camp.

A prayer in its simplest definition is merely
a wish turned Godward.

> PHILLIPS BROOKS

My words fly up; my thoughts remain below;
Words without thoughts never to heaven go.

> WILLIAM SHAKESPEARE
> *Hamlet*

May the wisdom of God instruct me, the
eye of God watch over me, the ear of God
hear me, the word of God give me sweet
talk, the hand of God defend me, the way
of God guide me.

Christ be with me.
Christ before me.
Christ in me.
Christ under me.
Christ over me.
Christ on my right hand.
Christ on my left hand.
Christ on this side.
Christ on that side.

Christ in the head of everyone to whom I speak.
Christ in the mouth of every person who speaks to me.
Christ in the eye of every person who looks upon me.
Christ in the ear of everyone who hears me today.
Amen.

SAINT PATRICK

HOW GOD ANSWERS

He prayed for strength that he might achieve;
He was made weak that he might obey.
He prayed for wealth that he might do greater things;
He was given infirmity that he might do better things.
He prayed for riches that he might be happy;
He was given poverty that he might be wise.
He prayed for power that he might have the praise of men;
He was given infirmity that he might feel the need of God.
He prayed for all things that he might enjoy life;
He was given life that he might enjoy all things.
He had received nothing that he asked for—all that he hoped for;
His prayer was answered—he was most blessed.

AUTHOR UNKNOWN

All things, whatsoever ye shall ask in
prayer, believing, ye shall receive.

Matthew 21:22

The time of business does not with me
differ from the time of prayer; and in the
noise and clatter of my kitchen, while
several persons are at the same time calling
for different things, I possess God in as
great tranquillity as if I were upon my
knees . . . . We should establish ourselves
in a sense of God's presence by continually
conversing with him.

BROTHER LAWRENCE
The Practice of the Presence of God

Tell God all that is in your heart, as one unloads one's heart to a dear friend. People who have no secrets from each other never want subjects of conversation; they do not weigh their words, because there is nothing to be kept back. Neither do they seek for something to say; they talk out of the abundance of their hearts, just what they think. Blessed are they who attain to such familiar, unreserved intercourse with God.

FRANCQIS DE FÉNELON

Be not forgetful of prayer.
     Every time you pray, if your prayer is sincere,
there will be new feeling and new meaning in it,
          which will give you fresh courage,
          and you will understand that prayer is
          an education.

FËDOR DOSTOEVSKI

Prayer is the wing wherewith the soul flies to heaven, and meditation the eye where-with we see God.

SAINT AMBROSE

My mother was not a sentimental parent. In many ways she was a Spartan. But one of my strongest childhood experiences is of Mother going to a room she kept for the purpose on the third floor to pray. She spent hours in prayer, often beginning before dawn. When we asked her advice about anything, she would say, "I must ask God first."

MADAME CHIANG KAI-SHEK

OCCASIONS FOR PRAYER

It has now become a habit with me to pray every time I see a funeral procession. Even though I do not know who it is, I know that in the cars behind that hearse are some saddened hearts that especially need help. It is not hard for me to pray, "Father, may just now that family especially feel the presence of the sympathizing Jesus."

I always pray when I pass a church building. No matter what denomination it is, people meet in that place to worship God and to gain inspiration for Christian service. Some people stand off and criticize the church, but I know that my community is better because that church is there, so it comes naturally to me to pray for it.

When I see one in the uniform of our country, I am led to say a prayer. On some battlefield that boy or girl may lose his or her life defending me and all I hold dear. I think of the mother and father whose hearts are anxious. Maybe there are a young wife and some little children back home. Prayer for one in service comes very quickly to me. I especially pray that away from home that boy might above all things hold high his standards.

Of course, I always pray for the sick. I pray that God might direct the mind and guide the hand of the physician. I ask a special blessing on the nurse who has such a difficult job yet one so very important. And I pray that the Great Physician might have a definite part in the case.

CHARLES L. ALLEN

Grant me, O Lord, to know what I ought to know,
to love what I ought to love,
to praise what delights Thee most,
to value what is precious in Thy sight,
to hate what is offensive to Thee.
Do not suffer me to judge according to the sight
    of my eyes,
nor to pass sentence according to the hearing
    of the ears of ignorant men;
but to discern with a true judgment
    between things visible and spiritual,
and above all, always to inquire what is
    the good pleasure of Thy will.

THOMAS À KEMPIS

Prayer is the contemplation of the facts of life from the highest point of view.

RALPH WALDO EMERSON

Who riseth from prayer a better man, his prayer is answered.

GEORGE MEREDITH

Your Father knoweth what things ye have need of, before ye ask him.

Matthew 6:8

Thank You, Father, for this moment of quiet, and for the strength to pick up my tasks again, renewed and refreshed because I have paused to be with You, for the sake of Jesus Christ our Lord. *Amen.*

SHERWOOD E. WIRT
The Quiet Corner

Prayer is the world in tune.

HENRY VAUGHN

God warms his hands at man's heart when he prays.

JOHN MASEFIELD

Give us, O Lord, steadfast hearts, which no unworthy thought can drag downwards; unconquered hearts, which no tribulation can wear out, upright hearts, which no unworthy purpose may tempt aside. Bestow upon us also, O Lord our God, understanding to know Thee, diligence to seek Thee, wisdom to find Thee, and a faithfulness that may finally embrace Thee.

THOMAS AQUINAS

. . . More things are wrought by prayer
Than this world dreams of. Wherefore, let thy voice
Rise like a fountain for me night and day.
For what are men better than sheep or goats
That nourish a blind life within the brain,
If, knowing God, they lift not hands of prayer
Both for themselves and those who call them friend?
For so the whole round earth is every way
Bound by gold chains about the feet of God . . . .

ALFRED TENNYSON
Morte D'Arthur

O Holy Spirit of God, abide with us;
inspire all our thoughts;
pervade our imaginations;
suggest all our decisions;
order all our doings.

Be with us in our silence and in our speech,
in our haste and in our leisure,
in company and in solitude,
in the freshness of the morning and in the
        weariness of the evening;
and give us grace at all times humbly to
        rejoice in Thy mysterious companionship.

JOHN BAILLIE

Did not God
Sometimes withhold in mercy what we ask,
We should be ruined at our own request.

HANNAH MORE

I have lived to thank God that all my
prayers have not been answered.

JEAN INGELOW

God has not always answered my prayers.
If He had, I would have married the wrong
man—several times!

RUTH BELL GRAHAM

I have been driven many times to my knees
by the overwhelming conviction that I had
nowhere else to go.

ABRAHAM LINCOLN

THE FAVORITE PRAYER OF PRESIDENT TRUMAN

Almighty and Everlasting God, Creator of Heaven, Earth and the Universe:

Help me to be, to think, to act what is right, because it is right; make me truthful, honest and honorable in all things; make me intellectually honest for the sake of right and honor, and without thought of reward to me. Give me the ability to be charitable, forgiving and patient with my fellowmen—help me to understand their motives and their shortcomings—even as Thou understandest mine!

Amen, Amen, Amen.

Personal prayer, it seems to me, is one of the simplest necessities of life, as basic to the individual as sunshine, food and water—and at times, of course, more so. By prayer I believe we mean an effort to get in touch with the Infinite. We know that our prayers are imperfect. Of course they are. We are imperfect human beings. A thousand experiences have convinced me beyond room of doubt that prayer multiplies the strength of the individual and brings within the scope of his capabilities almost any conceivable objective.

DWIGHT D. EISENHOWER

O Lord, Thou knowest how busy I must be
this day. If I forget Thee, do not forget me.

LORD ASHLEY before the
Battle of Edge Hill

There are times in a man's life when, re-
gardless of the attitude of the body, the
soul is on its knees in prayer.

VICTOR HUGO

A TEACHER'S PRAYER

God, give me wisdom, let me understand
That I may teach the needful thing;
Help me to see the hidden, stranger child,
That I life's rightful messages may bring.

God give me patience for the endless task,
The daily repetitions, the slow years
Of molding, line by line, the human mind,
Until at length 'tis free from sordid fears.

God, let me care for those whom I must teach;
Like the great Teacher let me ever love
With tender, brooding, understanding heart,
Eyes wise, farseeing as the stars above.

God, give me faith to see beyond today,
To sow the seed and cultivate the soil;
Then wait serenely, trusting in thy power,
To bless and multiply my humble toil.

AUTHOR UNKNOWN

If you would never cease to pray, never
cease to long for it. The continuance of your
longing is the continuance of your prayer.

SAINT AUGUSTINE

The privilege of prayer to me is one of the most cherished possessions because faith and experience alike convince me that God Himself sees and answers, and His answers I never venture to criticize. It is only my part to ask. It is entirely His to give or withhold, as He knows is best. If it were otherwise, I would not dare to pray at all. In the quiet of home, in the heat of life and strife, in the face of death, the privilege of speech with God is inestimable. I value it more because it calls for nothing that the wayfaring man, though a fool, cannot give—that is, the simplest expression to his simplest desire. When I can neither see, nor hear, nor speak, still I can pray so that God can hear. When I finally pass through the valley of the shadow of death, I expect to pass through it in conversation with Him.

SIR WILFRED GRENFELL

FOR A FRIEND

I don't believe I've ever thought to thank you, God, for this wonderful friend. But I do thank you for creating her and letting her enrich my life this way.

Thank you for all the years we've known each other and the confidences and hopes and troubles that we've shared.

Thank you for the understanding we bring to each other. For the patience we have with each other's faults; for the advice and even the scoldings we are able to give each other without either of us taking offense.

Thank you for the help we have been to each other—in this way, and so many more. Thank you that because of her I am a better, happier person, and that she has grown as a person too because of me.

Thank you that she would give me anything in her power—time, money, work, possessions, encouragement, sympathy—whatever my need. And that she knows I would be as quick to respond to whatever her needs might be.

Thank you that we can laugh together, cry together, rejoice together. And although we may not see each other for a long time, when we do come together it is always the same.

Lord, bless and keep her, this person you fashioned and filled with qualities that have meant so much to me. Lord, thank you for my friend.

MARJORIE HOLMES
I've Got to Talk to Somebody, God

Prayer should be the key of the day and the lock of the night.

THOMAS FULLER

Lord Jesus, merciful and patient, grant us grace, I beseech Thee, ever to teach in a teachable spirit; learning along with those we teach, and learning from them whenever Thou so pleasest. Word of God, speak to us, speak by us, what Thou wilt. Wisdom of God, instruct us, instruct by us, if and whom Thou wilt. Eternal Truth, reveal Thyself to us, in whatever measure Thou wilt; that we and they may all be taught of God.

CHRISTINA G. ROSSETTI

Now I lay me down to sleep,
I pray Thee, Lord, Thy child to keep;
Thy love go with me all the night
And wake me with the morning light.

AUTHOR UNKNOWN

What joy I have in being able to come directly to You, Lord, in prayer. You know my every thought and longing and my heart is filled with love and thankfulness to You. In Jesus' name, amen.

—J. W. B.

Joy

Joy is the gigantic secret of the Christian.
—G. K. CHESTERTON

People wondered as they saw the blind child playing so happily—she seemed to radiate a joy to others around her. Fanny Crosby was blinded when just a small baby by a doctor's administering a wrong medication. Her mother grieved to think of the dark world her little girl would know.

Fanny had an inner joy that completely compensated for her blindness—it was the joy of Christ in her life. At eight years of age she wrote:

> O what a happy soul am I!
> Although I cannot see,
> I am resolved that in this world
> Contented I will be;
> How many blessings I enjoy
> That other people don't!
> To weep and sigh because I'm blind,
> I cannot, and I won't.

Often she would say, "Don't waste sympathy on me—I'm the happiest person alive!" She married a blind Methodist clergyman. They had a child who died as an infant. All her sorrow and victory were poured into her hymns. Whenever Fanny wrote she would kneel in prayer first and then the words would come spontaneously. During her life she wrote thousands of hymns which have been sung all over the world. The blind, joyous woman would always hold a small Testament when she spoke in public. "It gives me strength for the task," she would say. Having accepted completely her blindness, she never longed to see, for "the first time I do I want to see my Saviour's face."

The night before she died, at the age of ninety-five, she wrote the following verses to parents in the neighborhood who had just lost a child:

You will reach the river brink
Some sweet day, by and by
You will find your broken link
Some sweet day, by and by.

O the loved ones waiting there
By the tree of life so fair
Till you come their joy to share
Some sweet day, by and by.

The beloved hymnwriter was buried in Bridgeport, Connecticut. The grave-stone was simply engraved AUNT FANNY and to the side SHE HATH DONE WHAT SHE COULD. These words of Jesus recall the joy that she still brings to so many through her inspiring writings.

—J. W. B.

I have learned, in whatsoever state I am,
therewith to be content.

Philippians 4:11

Where your pleasure is, there is your treasure.
Where your treasure is, there is your heart.
Where your heart is, there is your happiness.

SAINT AUGUSTINE

The measure of a happy life is not from the
fewer or more suns we behold, the fewer or
more breaths we draw, or meals we repeat,
but from having once lived well, acted our
part handsomely, and made our exit cheer-
fully.

LORD SHAFTESBURY

I WANDERED LONELY AS A CLOUD

I wandered lonely as a cloud
  That floats on high o'er vales and hills,
When all at once I saw a crowd,
  A host of golden daffodils.
Beside the lake, beneath the trees,
Fluttering and dancing in the breeze.

The waves beside them danced; but they
  Out-did the sparkling waves in glee;
A poet could not but be gay
  In such a jocund company:
I gazed—and gazed—but little thought
What wealth the show to me had brought.
For oft, when on my couch I lie
  In vacant or in pensive mood,
They flash upon that inward eye
  Which is the bliss of solitude;
And then my heart with pleasure fills
And dances with the daffodils.

              WILLIAM WORDSWORTH

Delight thyself . . . in the Lord; and he
shall give thee the desires of thine heart.
Commit thy way unto the Lord; trust also
in him; and he shall bring it to pass. And
he shall bring forth thy righteousness as
the light, and thy judgment as the noon-
day. Rest in the Lord and wait patiently for
him . . . .

              Psalms 37:4–7

The only ones among you who will be
really happy are those who will have
sought and found how to serve.

              ALBERT SCHWEITZER

THE SHEPHERD'S SONG

He that is down needs fear no fall,
  He that is low, no pride;
He that is humble ever shall
  Have God to be his guide.

I am content with what I have,
  Little be it or much:
And, Lord, contentment still I crave,
  Because Thou savest such.

Fulness to such a burden is
That go on pilgrimage:
Here little, and hereafter bliss,
Is best from age to age.
                        JOHN BUNYAN
                        Pilgrim's Progress

Those who bring sunshine into the lives of
others cannot keep it from themselves.
                        SIR JAMES M. BARRIE

I HAVE FOUND SUCH JOY

I have found such joy in simple things;
A plain clean room, a nut-brown loaf of bread,
A cup of milk, a kettle as it sings,
The shelter of a roof above my head,
And in a leaf-laced square along a floor,
Where yellow sunlight glimmers through a
        door.

I have found such joy in things that fill
My quiet days: a curtain's blowing grace,
A potted plant upon my window sill,
A rose fresh-cut and placed within a vase,
A table cleared, a lamp beside a chair,
And books I long have loved beside me there.
                        GRACE NOLL CROWELL

Happiness is a perfume you cannot pour
on others without getting a few drops on
yourself.
                        RALPH WALDO EMERSON

For ye shall go out with joy, and be led
forth with peace: the mountains and the
hills shall break forth before you into singing, and all the trees of the field shall clap
their hands.
                        Isaiah 55:12

The soul's joy lies in doing.

PERCY BYSSHE SHELLEY

Cheerfulness and content are great beau-
tifiers and are famous preservers of youth-
ful looks.

CHARLES DICKENS

There are two ways of being happy; we may either diminish our
wants or augment our means. Either will do, the result is the same. And
it is for each man to decide for himself, and do that which happens to be
the easiest. If you are idle or sick or poor, however hard it may be for
you to diminish your wants, it will be harder to augment your means. If
you are active and prosperous or young or in good health, it may be
easier for you to augment your means than to diminish your wants. But
if you are wise, you will do both at the same time, young or old, rich or
poor, sick or well. And if you are very wise, you will do both in such a
way as to augment the general happiness of society.

BENJAMIN FRANKLIN

Most folks are about as happy as they make
up their minds to be.

ABRAHAM LINCOLN

Thou wilt shew me the path of life: in thy
presence is fulness of joy; at thy right hand
there are pleasures for evermore.

Psalms 16:11

He that comforts all that mourn
Shall to joy your sorrow turn:
Joy to know your sins forgiven,
Joy to keep the way to heaven,
Joy to win his welcome grace,
Joy to see Him face to face.

CHARLES WESLEY

Godliness with contentment is great gain.

1 Timothy 6:6

Happy the man, and happy he alone,
He who can call to-day his own;
He who, secure within, can say,
"To-morrow, do thy worst, for I have liv'd to-day.
Be fair or foul, or rain or shine,
The joys I have possessed, in spite of fate, are mine.
Not heaven itself upon the past has power;
But what has been, has been, and I have had my hour."
                                        JOHN DRYDEN
                                        "Imitation of Horace"

Happiness is a butterfly, which, when pur-
sued, is always just beyond your grasp, but
which, if you will sit down quietly, may
alight upon you.
                    NATHANIEL HAWTHORNE

Mirth is God's medicine. Everybody ought
to bathe in it. Grim care, moroseness,
anxiety—all this rust of life ought to be
scoured off by the oil of mirth. It is better
than emery. Every man ought to rub himself with it. A man without mirth is like a
wagon without springs, in which everyone
is caused disagreeably to jolt by every peb-
ble over which it runs.
                    HENRY WARD BEECHER

The true secret of happiness lies in the taking a genuine interest in all the details of
daily life.
                    WILLIAM MORRIS

He is a wise man who does not grieve for
the things which he has not, but rejoices
for those which he has.
                    EPICTETUS

Written on the flyleaf of a Bible by George
V: "The secret of happiness is not to do
what you like to do, but to learn to like
what you have to do."

He looks on my life in tenderness for He loves me deeply. He sees the long years during which His goodness and mercy have followed me without slackening. He longs to see some measure of that same goodness and mercy not only passed on to others by me but also passed back to Him with joy.

He longs for love—my love.

And I love Him—only and because He first loved me.

Then He is satisfied.

W. PHILLIP KELLER
A Shepherd Looks at Psalm 23

My crown is in my heart, not on my head;
Not deck'd with diamonds and Indian stones,
Nor to be seen: my crown is call'd content;
A crown it is that seldom kings enjoy.

WILLIAM SHAKESPEARE
King Henry VI

Money may buy the husk of things, but not the kernel. It brings you food but not appetite, medicine but not health, acquaintances but not friends, servants but not faithfulness, days of joy but not peace or happiness.

HENRIK IBSEN

If one only wished to be happy, this could be easily accomplished; but we wish to be happier than other people, and this is always difficult, for we believe others to be happier than they are.

MONTESQUIEU

I am not bound to make the world go right,
But only to discover and to do,
With cheerful heart, the work that God appoints.

JEAN INGELOW

Oh, the wild joys of living! the leaping from rock up to rock.
The strong rending of boughs from the firtree, the cool silver shock
Of the plunge in a pool's living water, the hunt of the bear,
And the sultriness showing the lion is couched in his lair.
How good is man's life, the mere living! How fit to employ
All the heart and the soul and the senses for ever in joy!
ROBERT BROWNING

I like the laughter that opens the lips and
the heart, that shows at the same time
pearls and the soul.
VICTOR HUGO

. . . God hath made me to laugh, so that
all that hear will laugh with me.
Genesis 21:6

A characteristic of the great saints is their
power of levity. Angels can fly because
they can take themselves lightly. One "set-
tles down" into a sort of selfish serious-
ness; but one has to rise to a gay self-
forgetfulness. A man falls into a "brown
study"; he reaches up to a blue sky.
G. K. CHESTERTON

Give me a sense of humor, Lord;
Give me the grace to see a joke,
To get some happiness from life,
And pass it on to other folk.
Inscription on Chester Cathedral

This is a cheerful world as I see it from my garden under the shadows
of my vines. But if I were to ascend some high mountain and look out
over the wide lands, you know very well what I should see: brigands on
the highways, pirates on the sea, armies fighting, cities burning; in the
amphitheaters men murdered to please applauding crowds; selfishness
and cruelty and misery and despair under all roofs. It is a bad world,
Donatus, an incredibly bad world. But I have discovered in the midst of
it a quiet and holy people who have learned a great secret. They have

found a joy which is a thousand times better than any pleasure of our sinful life. They are despised and persecuted, but they care not. They are masters of their souls. They have overcome the world. These people, Donatus, are the Christians—and I am one of them.

SAINT CYPRIAN (third-century martyr)

They might not need me, yet they might.
I'll let my head be just in sight;
A smile as small as mine might be
Precisely their necessity.

EMILY DICKINSON

The hands of those I meet are dumbly eloquent to me. I have met people so empty of joy that when I clasped their frosty fingertips it seemed as if I were shaking hands with a northeast storm. Others there are whose hands have sunbeams in them, so that their grasp warms my heart. It may be only the clinging touch of a child's hand, but there is as much potential sunshine in it for me as there is in a loving glance for others.

HELEN KELLER
The Story of My Life

Peace does not mean the end of all our striving,
    Joy does not mean the drying of our tears;
Peace is the power that comes to souls arriving
    Up to the light where God Himself appears.
Joy is the wine that God is ever pouring
    Into the hearts of those who strive with Him,
Light'ning their eyes to vision and adoring,
    Strength'ning their arms to warfare glad and grim.

G. A. STUDDERT-KENNEDY

Happiness is the full use of your powers
along lines of excellence in a life affording
scope.

JOHN F. KENNEDY
Profiles in Courage

When we cannot find contentment in ourselves, it is useless to seek it elsewhere.

FRANÇOIS DE LA ROCHEFOUCAULD

All the misfortunes of men spring from
their not knowing how to live quietly at
home in their own rooms.

BLAISE PASCAL

O Holy Spirit, descend plentifully into my
heart. Enlighten the dark corners of this
neglected dwelling and scatter there Thy
cheerful beams.

SAINT AUGUSTINE

*Father, my joy comes from knowing of Your love and in turn loving
You. There is nothing in the world that can compare with this!
Thank You, my Lord and my God. Amen.*

—J. W. B.

Nation

The love of liberty is the love of others,
The love of power is the love of ourselves.
—WILLIAM HAZLITT

The Civil War was raging and America was torn apart. President Lincoln had spent many sleepless nights, as the reports of the casualties on both sides reached the White House. Often the President would sit for hours, head in hands, thinking of the terrible carnage that the nation was experiencing.

As the burdens of war grew almost unbearable, anti-slavery supporters visited the White House to encourage the President. One of these was Julia Ward Howe, co-editor of the *Boston Commonwealth*. She was asked to tour the Union Army camps with President Lincoln. It was a tragic sight—so many weary men torn from battle, some only young boys. The light from the camp fires seemed to deepen the lines of fatigue on their faces. In spite of all they had suffered, the men sang and the tune "John Brown" echoed throughout the camps. It was a southern song, yet the northern troops found it comforting.

On returning to her hotel room in Washington, Julia Ward Howe could not forget the haunting melody. Unable to sleep because of the memory of the suffering men, she began to compose sorrowful and triumphant words to the tune.

Even in the midst of the terrible Civil War, "Battle Hymn of the Republic" became a symbol of a basic unity between both sides—a southern tune with northern words.

Mrs. Howe received only five dollars for allowing the *Atlantic Monthly* to print the words to the song. "Battle Hymn of the Republic" has since been sung, however, at presidential inaugurations, State funerals, and by millions of Americans, from both North and South, who have wanted to express their love for this great nation of free men and women.

—*J. W. B.*

BATTLE HYMN OF THE REPUBLIC

Mine eyes have seen the glory of the coming of the Lord;
He is trampling out the vintage where the grapes of wrath are stored;
He hath loosed the fateful lightning of His terrible, swift sword;
　His truth is marching on.

I have seen Him in the watch-fires of a hundred circling camps;
They have builded Him an altar in the evening dews and damps;
I can read His righteous sentence by the dim and flaring lamps:
　His day is marching on.

He has sounded forth the trumpet that shall never call retreat;
He is sifting out the hearts of men before His judgment-seat:
O be swift, my soul, to answer Him! be jubilant, my feet!
　Our God is marching on.

In the beauty of the lilies Christ was born across the sea,
With a glory in His bosom that transfigures you and me;
As He died to make men holy, let us die to make men free,
　While God is marching on.

                                                    JULIA WARD HOWE

With malice toward none;
With charity for all;
With firmness in the right, as God gives us to see
　　the right,
Let us strive on to finish the work we are in;
To bind up the nation's wounds;
To care for him who shall have borne the battle,
And for his widow,
And his orphan—
To do all which may achieve and cherish a just and
　　lasting peace among ourselves,
And with all nations.

                                   ABRAHAM LINCOLN
                                   (from the Second Inaugural
                                   Address, March 4, 1865)

We must have many Lincoln-hearted men.
                                   VACHEL LINDSAY

Blessed is the nation whose God is the Lord . . . .
Psalms 33:12

And have we now forgotten that powerful Friend? Or do we imagine we no longer need His assistance? I have lived a long time; and the longer I live, the more convincing proofs I see of this truth: that God governs in the affairs of men. And if a sparrow cannot fall to the ground without His notice, is it probable that an empire can rise without His aid?

BENJAMIN FRANKLIN

History is "the track of God's footsteps through time." It is in His dealings with our forefathers that we may expect to find the laws by which He will deal with us.

CHARLES KINGSLEY

I know there is a Supreme Being who rules the affairs of men and whose goodness and mercy have always followed the American people, and I know He will not turn from us now if we humbly and reverently seek His powerful aid.

GROVER CLEVELAND

I do not believe there is a problem in this country or the world today which could not be settled if approached through the teaching of the Sermon on the Mount.

HARRY S TRUMAN

God grant that not only the love of liberty but a thorough knowledge of the rights of man may pervade all the nations of the earth, so that a philosopher may set his foot anywhere on its surface and say: "This is my country!"

BENJAMIN FRANKLIN

I desire no future
that will break
the ties of the past.

GEORGE ELIOT

Before all else we seek, upon our common
    labor as a nation, the blessings of Almighty
    God. And the hopes in our hearts fashion
    the deepest prayers of our whole people.
May we pursue the right—without self-righteousness.
May we know unity—without conformity.
May we grow in strength—without pride in self.
May we, in our dealings with all peoples of the earth,
    ever speak truth and serve justice.
May the light of freedom, coming to all darkened
    lands, flame brightly—until at last the darkness
    is no more.
May the turbulence of our age yield to a true
    time of peace, when men and nations share a life that
    honors the dignity of each, the brotherhood of all.

DWIGHT D. EISENHOWER

A NATION'S STRENGTH

What makes a nation's pillars high
    And its foundations strong?
What makes it mighty to defy
    The foes that round it throng?

It is not gold. Its kingdoms grand
    Go down in battle shock;
Its shafts are laid on sinking sand,
    Not on abiding rock.

Is it the sword? Ask the red dust
    Of empires passed away;
The blood has turned their stones to rust,
    Their glory to decay.

And is it pride? Ah, that bright crown
    Has seemed to nations sweet;
But God has struck its luster down
    In ashes at His feet.

Not gold but only men can make
  A people great and strong;
Men who for truth and honor's sake
  Stand fast and suffer long.

Brave men who work while others sleep,
  Who dare while others fly—
They build a nation's pillars deep
  And lift them to the sky.

              RALPH WALDO EMERSON

In the future days, which we seek to make secure,
  we look forward to a world founded upon four
  essential human freedoms.
The first is freedom of speech and expression
  —everywhere in the world.
The second is freedom of every person to worship
  God in his own way—everywhere in the world.
The third is freedom from want—which, translated
  into world terms, means economic understanding
  which will secure to every nation a healthy
  peacetime life for its inhabitants—everywhere
  in the world.
The fourth is freedom from fear—which, translated
  into world terms, means a world-wide reduction
  of armaments to such a point and in such a fashion
  that no nation will be in a position to commit an
  act of physical aggression against any neighbor—
  anywhere in the world.

              FRANKLIN D. ROOSEVELT

When an American says that he loves his
country, he means not only that he loves
the New England hills, the prairies glisten-
ing in the sun, the wide and rising plains,
the great mountains, and the sea. He
means that he loves an inner air, an inner
light in which freedom lives and in which a
man can draw the breath of self-respect.

          ADLAI STEVENSON

I see that patriotism is not enough. I must
die without hatred or bitterness toward
anyone.

EDITH CAVELL
(English nurse shot by Germans
as a spy in World War I)

And so, my fellow Americans, ask not what
your country can do for you; ask what you
can do for your country.

JOHN F. KENNEDY

ONE PURE SOURCE

The meaning of our word America flows
from one pure source. Within the soul of
America is the freedom of mind and spirit
in man. Here alone are the open windows
through which pours the sunlight of all the
human spirit. Here alone human dignity is
not a dream but a major accomplishment.

HERBERT HOOVER

Raised in liberty, most Americans accept
their freedom as a matter of course. Sometimes it seems to me you free people don't
realize what you've got . . . You can wake
up in the morning free to do as you choose,
to read what you wish, to worship the way
you please, and to listen to a lovely piece of
music.

JAN MASARYK
Czechoslovakian Statesman

MOUNT VERNON INSCRIPTION

Washington, the brave, the wise, the good,
Supreme in war, in council, and in peace.
Valiant without ambition, discreet without fear,
Confident without presumption.
In disaster, calm; in success, moderate; in all, himself.

The hero, the patriot, the Christian.
The father of nations, the friend of mankind,
Who, when he had won all, renounced all,
And sought in the bosom of his family and of nature,
    retirement,
And in the hope of religion, immortality.

Nothing that is morally wrong can be polit-
ically right.

PRIME MINISTER WILLIAM GLADSTONE

THE HOMELAND

I vow to thee, my country, all earthly things above
Entire and whole and perfect, the service of my love.
The love that asks no questions; the love that stands
    the test,
That lays upon the altar the dearest and the best;
The love that never falters, the love that pays the price;
The love that makes undaunted the final sacrifice.

And there's another country I've heard of long ago,
Most dear to them that love her, most great to them that know.
We may not count her armies, we may not see her King;
Her fortress is a faithful heart, her pride is suffering.
And soul by soul and silently her shining bounds increase,
And her ways are ways of gentleness and all her paths
    are peace. *Amen.*

SIR CECIL SPRING-RICE
British Ambassador to the United States
(written the night before his return
to England knowing he was fatally ill)

"General, we are lost; everything is lost," said a staff officer
to Washington during a difficult period of the Revolutionary
War.

"Sir, you do not know the resources and genius of liberty,"
Washington replied.

PLYMOUTH ROCK INSCRIPTION

This spot marks the final resting-place of the Pilgrims of the *Mayflower*. In weariness and hunger and in cold, fighting the wilderness and burying their dead in common graves that the Indians should not know how many had perished, they here laid the foundations of a state in which all men for countless ages should have liberty to worship God in their own way. All ye who pass by and see this stone remember, and dedicate yourselves anew to the resolution that you will not rest until this lofty ideal shall have been realized throughout the earth.

Breathes there the man, with soul so dead,
Who never to himself hath said,
   This is my own, my native land!
Whose heart hath ne'er within him burn'd,
As home his footsteps he hath turn'd
   From wandering on a foreign strand!
If such there breathe, go, mark him well;
For him no Minstrel raptures swell;
High though his titles, proud his name,
Boundless his wealth as wish can claim;
Despite those titles, power, and pelf,
The wretch, concentered all in self,
Living, shall forfeit fair renown,
And, doubly dying, shall go down
To the vile dust from whence he sprung,
Unwept, unhonor'd, and unsung.

SIR WALTER SCOTT
The Lay of the Last Minstrel

Thank You, Almighty God, for this nation. Help me to realize each day all that has been sacrificed over the years so that I may live in freedom. Help me remember the cost and never take this privilege for granted. May the life I live show my love both for You and my country. Amen. —*J. W. B.*

Character

When a man's fight begins with himself,
He is worth something.
                        —ROBERT BROWNING

The man described as the best-loved missionary of Colonial America was David Brainerd, the Beloved Yankee. His life showed the absolute integrity of his character—honest, kind, resolute, compassionate, and above all, completely dedicated to serving his Saviour, Jesus Christ.

Hezekiah and Dorothy Brainerd's son David grew up with his nine brothers and sisters in a country home close to the Connecticut River. Their lives were kept busy with farm chores, school lessons, Bible study, and church attendance. David prayed often and hoped he was converted, but there did not seem to be any joy or assurance in his life. He began in his teenage years to search for the real meaning of life in earnest, seeking out the counsel of older people. He read and re-read the Bible and spent as much time as he could attending church. "In short," he said, "I had a very good *outside*."

Finally, after great inner turmoil, he had an experience that gave him the peace he had been searching for; walking in the woods on a Sunday evening, he came to a realization of Christ's love for him and he wondered why all the world did not see "this lovely, blessed and excellent way." There was now a light within his soul and a dedication to his Lord, which led him to become a missionary to the Indians, riding many hundreds of miles on horseback through New York, New Jersey, and Pennsylvania.

During this time he met and fell in love with Jerusha Edwards, the beautiful daughter of Rev. Jonathan Edwards. After they were engaged, David had to tell her that he could not go through with the marriage, because of his work for God. He gave himself completely to the Indians, and even though he was in ill health, he would ride hundreds of miles to be with his beloved people. His love and concern for the Indians was what made them want to listen to his preaching. It was not an unusual sight to see him with his sleeves rolled up helping build fences, while he told them of God's love for each one of them.

Jerusha, whom he still loved, nursed him in his final illness. The Sunday before he died he whispered to her: "Jerusha, if I thought I should not see you, and be happy with you in another world, I could not bear to part with you . . . We shall spend a happy eternity together." A few days later, at the age of twenty-nine, he died—Jerusha dying only four months later.

On David Brainerd's grave is inscribed: A FAITHFUL AND LABORIOUS MISSIONARY—on Jerusha's, next to his: I SHALL BE SATISFIED WHEN I AWAKE WITH THY LIKENESS. The Indians had often heard these words preached by their beloved "Yankee," and it was because they saw in his life the likeness of Christ that so many came to know Him.

—J. W. B.

He was a young man, —he was a lovely man; he was a staff to walk with . . . He slept on a deer-skin or a bear-skin. He ate bearmeat and samp: then we knew he was not proud. He would come to my grandmother and say, "I am hungry—make haste!" Then she would take down the kettle, and he would eat. But some of the people did not like him, and said, "What has this white man come here for? We don't want him here!" and they told him to go off . . . After a while they found he was an honest man and then they would do anything he said.

A Delaware Indian woman
(a convert of Brainerd's)

Good actions are the invisible hinges on the doors of heaven.

VICTOR HUGO

Blessed is the man that walketh not in the counsel
of the ungodly, nor standeth in the way of sinners,
nor sitteth in the seat of the scornful.
But his delight is in the law of the Lord; and in his
law doth he meditate day and night.

And he shall be like a tree planted by the rivers
of water, that bringeth forth his fruit in his
season; his leaf also shall not wither; and whatsoever he doeth shall prosper.

Psalms 1:1–3

Thoughtfulness is the beginning of great
sanctity. If you learn this art of being
thoughtful, you will become more and
more Christlike for His heart was meek and
He always thought of others. Jesus went
about doing good. Mary, His mother, did
nothing else in Cana but thought of the
needs of others and made their needs
known to Jesus.

MOTHER TERESA

All treasures of wisdom and truth and
holiness are in God.
Through constant fellowship with Christ
true Christian character takes shape
within the soul. Therefore, pray for:
The grace of a thankful and uncomplaining
heart;
The grace of courage, whether in suffering
or in danger;
The grace of boldness in standing for what
is right;
The grace of bodily discipline;
The grace of strict truthfulness;
The grace of charity—refraining from hasty
judgments;
The grace of silence—refraining from hasty
speech;
The grace of forgiveness toward all who wrong
us;
The grace of tenderness toward all who are weak;
The grace of steadfastness in continuing to
desire and to pray.

JOHN BAILLIE

Character is what you are in the dark.

DWIGHT L. MOODY

I thank God for my handicaps, for, through
them, I have found myself, my work, and
my God.

HELEN KELLER

Good name in man and woman, dear my lord,
Is the immediate jewel of their souls:
Who steals my purse steals trash; 'tis something, nothing;
'Twas mine, 'tis his, and has been slave to thousands;
But he that filches from me my good name
Robs me of that which not enriches him,
And makes me poor indeed.

WILLIAM SHAKESPEARE
Othello

THE CHRISTIAN GENTLEMAN

A Christian gentleman will be slow to lose patience—a Christian grace.

A Christian gentleman will look for a way to be constructive, even when provoked.

A Christian gentleman will not envy the good fortune of others.

A Christian gentleman will refrain from trying to impress others with his own importance.

A Christian gentleman will have good manners.

A Christian gentleman will not be "touchy," even when he feels the right of resentment.

A Christian gentleman will think the best, not the worst of others; he will try to be as wise as the serpent and harmless as a dove in handling others.

A Christian gentleman will not gloat over the wickedness of other people.

Above all else, a Christian gentleman will exhibit the love of Christ in his heart and life.

L. NELSON BELL

You will find, as you look back upon your life, that the moments that stand out are the moments when you have done things for others.

HENRY DRUMMOND

To err is human; to forgive, divine.

ALEXANDER POPE

To reach the port of heaven we must sail, sometimes with the wind and sometimes against it—but we must sail, not drift or lie at anchor.

OLIVER WENDELL HOLMES

Never esteem anything as of advantage to thee that shall make thee break thy word or lose thy self-respect.

MARCUS AURELIUS

When you get into a tight place and everything goes against you, till it seems as though you could not hold on a minute longer, never give up then, for that is just the place and time that the tide will turn.

HARRIET BEECHER STOWE

One of the purest and most enduring of human pleasures is to be found in the possession of a good name among one's neighbors and acquaintances.

CHARLES W. ELIOT

Endeavor to be always patient of the faults and imperfections of others, for thou hast many faults and imperfections of thy own that require a reciprocation of forbearance. If thou art not able to make thyself that which thou wishest to be, how canst thou expect to mould another in conformity to thy will?

THOMAS À KEMPIS

Everyone is eagle-eyed to see another's
faults and deformity.

JOHN DRYDEN

I always seek the good that is in people
and leave the bad to Him who made mankind
and knows how to round off the corners.

GOETHE'S MOTHER

There is so much good in the worst of us,
And so much bad in the best of us,
That it ill behoves any of us
To find fault with the rest of us.

AUTHOR UNKNOWN

Speech is the index of the mind.

SENECA

Be not angry that you cannot make others
as you wish them to be, since you cannot
make yourself as you wish to be.

THOMAS À KEMPIS

Your disposition will be suitable to that
which you most frequently think on; for
the soul is, as it were, tinged with the color
and complexion of its own thoughts . . . .

Your life is what your thoughts make it.

MARCUS AURELIUS

The greatest pleasure I know is to do a good
action by stealth and to have it found out
by accident.

CHARLES LAMB

Goodness is the only investment that never
fails.

HENRY DAVID THOREAU

If there is any good that I can do or any kindness that I can show, let me do it quickly, for I shall not pass this way again.

PHILLIPS BROOKS

The man who does things makes many mistakes but he never makes the biggest mistake of all—doing nothing.

BENJAMIN FRANKLIN

He has the right to criticize who has the heart to help.

ABRAHAM LINCOLN

In this life, if you have anything to pardon, pardon quickly. Slow forgiveness is little better than no forgiveness.

SIR ARTHUR W. PINERO

Forget the slander you have heard,
Forget the hasty, unkind word;
Forget the quarrel and the cause,
Forget the whole affair, because
Forgetting is the only way.
Forget the storm of yesterday,
Forget the chap whose sour face
Forgets to smile in any place.
Forget you're not a millionaire,
Forget the gray streaks in your hair.
Forget the coffee when it's cold,
Forget to kick, forget to scold,
Forget the plumber's awful charge,
Forget the iceman's bill is large;
Forget the coalman and his ways,
Forget the winter's blustery days.

AUTHOR UNKNOWN

He who sows courtesy reaps friendship, and he who plants kindness.gathers love.

RICHARD BROOKS

If a man is interested in himself only, he is
very small; if he is interested in his family,
he is larger; if he is interested in his community, he is larger still.

                                        ARISTOTLE

    An apology
    Is a friendship preserver,
    Is often a debt of honor,
    Is never a sign of weakness,
    Is an antidote for hatred,
    Costs nothing but one's pride,
    Always saves more than it costs,
    Is a device needed in every home.

                              AUTHOR UNKNOWN

There is no more evil thing in this present
world than race prejudice, none at all! I
write deliberately—it is the worst single
thing in life now. It justifies and holds together more obscene cruelty and abomina-
tion than any other sort of error in the
world.

                                    H. G. WELLS

A hundred times every day I remind myself
that my inner and outer life depend on the
labors of other men, living and dead, and
that I must exert myself in order to give in
the same measure as I have received and
am still receiving.

                              ALBERT EINSTEIN

If we could read the secret history of our
enemies we should find in each man's life
sorrow and suffering enough to disarm all
hostility.

                HENRY WADSWORTH LONGFELLOW

I desire so to conduct the affairs of this administration that if at the end, when I come to lay down the reins of power, I have lost every other friend on earth, I shall at least have one friend left and that friend shall be down inside of me.

ABRAHAM LINCOLN

This above all: to thine own self be true,
And it must follow, as the night the day,
Thou canst not then be false to any man.

WILLIAM SHAKESPEARE
Hamlet

Difficulties are the things that show what men are.

EPICTETUS

Remember, what you possess in the world will be found at the day of your death to belong to someone else, but what you are will be yours forever.

HENRY VAN DYKE

My character, Lord Jesus, falls far short of the example You have given. May I live so close to You that this selfish life will completely radiate Your love for others. In Your name I pray, amen.

—J. W. B.

I am but one, but I am one; I cannot do
everything, but I can do something. What I can
do, by the grace of God, I will do.
—AUTHOR UNKNOWN

In gold letters inscribed on a huge black stone in Westminster Abbey are
carved the words: OTHER SHEEP I HAVE, WHICH ARE NOT OF THIS FOLD. The
tombstone is David Livingstone's.

As a young medical student, David Livingstone gave his life to God's service,
determined to work in whatever part of the world he was needed the most. He
first planned to become a missionary to China. However, when he heard the
words of Robert Moffatt of Africa, "From the hill where I live I can see the
smoke of a thousand villages where no Christian has ever gone," he was challenged to go to that great continent and dedicate his medical talent and his life
to alleviating the sufferings of so many, and to bring them the hope of the
Gospel of Christ.

When people asked him why he was going to Africa as a medical missionary,
David Livingstone answered: "God had an only Son, and He was a missionary
and a physician."

Years later, when an honorary degree was being bestowed upon him at a
Scottish university, it is said he stood with one arm hanging lifeless at his side
due to an injury from a battle with a lion. His face showed the years of hard and
unrelenting service—his skin was like leather from the African sun. The students, who were known to ridicule and mock previous recipients of honorary
degrees, rose in silent admiration as they watched this noble man receive an
accolade which was but a token of the stars in his crown waiting for him in
heaven.

Toward the end of his years, Livingstone beautifully described his life of
service:

People talk of the sacrifice I have made in spending so much of my life in Africa. Can that be called a sacrifice which is simply paid back as a small part of a great debt owing to our God, which we can never repay? Is that a sacrifice which brings its own best reward in healthful activity, the consciousness of doing good, peace of mind, and a bright hope of a glorious destiny hereafter? Away with the word in such a view, and with such a thought! It was emphatically no sacrifice. Say rather it is a privilege. Anxiety, sickness, suffering, or danger, now and then, with a foregoing of the common conveniences and charities of this life, may make us pause, and cause the spirit to waver and the soul to sink, but let this only be for a moment. All these are nothing when compared with the glory which shall hereafter be revealed in and for us. I never made a sacrifice. Of this we ought not to talk when we remember the great sacrifice which He made who left His Father's throne on high to give Himself for us.

—J. W. B.

DAVID LIVINGSTONE

He knew not that the trumpet he had blown
Out of the darkness of that dismal land
Had reached and roused an army of its own
To strike the chains from the slave's fettered hand.

Open the Abbey doors and bear him in
To sleep with kings and statesmen, chief and sage,
The missionary come of weaver-kin,
But great by work that brooks no lower wage.

He needs no epitaph to guard a name
Which men shall prize while worthy work is known;
He lived and died for good—be that his fame:
Let marble crumble, this is Living-stone.
>AUTHOR UNKNOWN—Lines from *Punch* on the
burial of Dr. Livingstone in Westminster Abbey

By many hands the work of God is done.
>RICHARD LE GALLIENNE

All service ranks the same with God.
. . . There is no last nor first.
>ROBERT BROWNING

DIVINE SERVICE CONDUCTED HERE THREE TIMES DAILY.
Motto above Mrs. Billy Graham's
kitchen sink

Always keep your eyes open for the little task, because it is the little task that is important to Jesus Christ. The future of the Kingdom of God does not depend on the enthusiasm of this or that powerful person; those great ones are necessary too, but it is equally necessary to have a great number of little people who will do a little thing in the service of Christ.

The great flowing rivers represent only a small part of all the water that is necessary to nourish and sustain the earth. Beside the flowing river there is the water in the earth—the subterranean water—and there are the little streams which continually enter the river and feed it and prevent it from sinking into the earth. Without these other waters—the silent hidden subterranean waters and the trickling streams—the great river could no longer flow. Thus it is with the little tasks to be fulfilled by us all.
>ALBERT SCHWEITZER

Have thy tools ready. God will find thee work.
>CHARLES KINGSLEY

We can do little things for God: I turn the cake that is frying in the pan for love of him, and that done, if there is nothing else to call me, I prostrate myself in worship before him who has given me Grace to work; afterwards I rise happier than a king.

BROTHER LAWRENCE

Unless a man undertakes more than he possibly can do he will never do all he can do.

HENRY DRUMMOND

No race can prosper till it learns that there is as much dignity in tilling a field as in writing a poem. It is at the bottom of life we must begin, and not at the top.

BOOKER T. WASHINGTON

Visitors to a factory in England during World War II would notice a man at a lathe who bore a striking resemblance to their king. It was, in fact, their king for each day after performing his official royal duties, the king of England would put on work clothes to work with his people.

No one is useless in this world who lightens the burden of it to anyone else.

CHARLES DICKENS

It is not the work we do, but the spirit within us that determines our real lives. If work is done in the spirit of consecration, it is just as sacred to sell soap as it is to preach sermons, or to be a butcher as it is to be a bishop. Your present work can be done for the glory of God—but there is something more to be said.

For every person who is faithful to the living of each day, there will come an hour of destiny—a time of self-fulfillment. It will come, I emphasize, if we remain faithful to the daily tasks without losing heart or hope. No member of God's team trains for the race without one day being given a chance to run. Sooner or later God says to every person who is ready, "Now—now your moment has come."

CHARLES L. ALLEN

Not what you possess but what you do
with what you have, determines your true
worth.

THOMAS CARLYLE

I used to ask God to help me. Then I asked
if I might help Him. I ended up by asking
Him to do His work through me.

HUDSON TAYLOR

Go ye therefore, and teach all nations, bap-
tizing them in the name of the Father, and
of the Son, and of the Holy Ghost:

Teaching them to observe all things whatsoever I have commanded you: and, lo, I
am with you alway, even unto the end of
the world.

Matthew 28:19, 20

SEND ME

Use me, God, in thy great harvest field,
Which stretcheth far and wide like a wide sea;
The gatherers are so few; I fear the precious yield
Will suffer loss. Oh, find a place for me!
A place where best the strength I have will tell:
It may be one the older toilers shun;
Be it a wide or narrow place, 'tis well
So that the work it holds be only done.

CHRISTINA G. ROSSETTI

In what way can I be of service to humanity? My time and energy belong to mankind.

LOUIS PASTEUR

I hope I will always keep my eyes on the King of kings, and Lord of lords, Jesus Christ. I pray that whether in singing or speaking or whatever I am doing I will desire only to please Him, that I may bask in *His* smile.

NORMA ZIMMER
Norma

The man who is born with a talent which he is meant to use finds his greatest happiness in using it.

JOHANN WOLFGANG VON GOETHE

It is only well with me when I have a chisel in my hand.

MICHELANGELO

When love and skill work together expect a masterpiece.

JOHN RUSKIN

Fritz Kreisler, the great violinist, once stated that he was born with music in his system—a gift of God. Knowing he did not acquire it, he felt he did not even deserve thanks for his music.

It is not fitting, when one is in God's service, to have a gloomy face or a chilling look.

SAINT FRANCIS OF ASSISI

God has had all there was of me. There have been men with greater brains than I, men with greater oppportunities. But from the day I got the poor of London on my heart and caught a vision of what Jesus Christ could do with them, on that day I made up my mind that God should have all of William Booth there was. And if there is anything of power in the Salvation Army today, it is because God has had all the adoration of my heart, all the power of my will, and all the influence of my life.

GENERAL WILLIAM BOOTH
Founder, Salvation Army

I am made of the stuff soldiers are made
from, but God willed it that my battle
should be one with medicine bottles and
pill boxes.

ROBERT LOUIS STEVENSON

If you sit down at set of sun
And count the acts that you have done,
  And, counting, find
One self-denying deed, one word
That eased the heart of him who heard—
  One glance most kind,
That fell like sunshine where it went—
Then you may count that day well spent.

GEORGE ELIOT

CONTENT

I was too ambitious in my deed,
And thought to distance all men in success,
Till God came on me, marked the place, and said,
"Ill-doer, henceforth keep within this line,
Attempting less than others"—and I stand
And work among Christ's little ones, content.

ELIZABETH BARRETT BROWNING

A man's work whether in music, painting,
or literature, is always a portrait of himself.

SAMUEL BUTLER

Johann Sebastian Bach wrote at the beginning of his compositions, "Only for the glory of God," and at the end, "With the help of Jesus Christ." Down through the years as his music has been played in the great cathedrals and the country churches throughout the world, people have been drawn closer to God and have been inspired to go out facing the tragedies and joys of their lives comforted and strengthened.

O God, we rejoice in being able to serve You! May our endeavors always reflect Your love and concern. Each day that is left of our earthly lives we would spend glorifying You, our Lord and our Redeemer. Amen.

—*J. W. B.*

Hope

The word which God has written
on the brow of every man is Hope.
—VICTOR HUGO

Several years ago a woman was rummaging through some old books in a little house in Ramsgate, England. Amongst them she found an old Bible, and blowing the dust from its cover she discovered embossed on it a Royal seal with the words: THE GIFT OF HER MAJESTY THE QUEEN—1842. The bold handwriting on the fly leaf, later to be confirmed as belonging to Queen Victoria, revealed it had been a gift to Delawarr, Lord Chamberlain.

In the Bible were old notes copied from the Scriptures and several Victorian bookmarks, some with long red ribbons. On one of the bookmarks was a very early photograph of Prince Albert, the Queen's husband, and embroidered in black were the words: I SHALL NOT IN THE GRAVE REMAIN.

Queen Victoria lived constantly with the hope that she would one day be reunited with Prince Albert. This hope was founded on her belief in Jesus Christ, and though she seemed to have many unorthodox views about religion, she never wavered in her hope of an afterlife because of Christ's sacrifice.

She had no illusions that her position in life automatically warranted her the right to enter heaven. She once wrote, "In after years God would not distinguish between the good life of a Crowned head or a peasant." Perhaps the most telling statement she ever made confirming her belief in Christ was, "Oh, I wish He would come today, so that I could lay my crowns at His feet!"

The favorite text of Queen Victoria was "Behold, now is the day of salvation," and at her funeral her most loved hymn was played—"Lead, Kindly Light," written by John Henry Newman. The last verse sums up what hope meant to her:

So long Thy power hath blest me, sure it still
  Will lead me on;
O'er moor and fen, o'er crag and torrent, till
  The night is gone;
And with the morn those angel faces smile,
Which I have loved long since, and lost awhile.

—*J. W. B.*

Looking for that blessed hope, and the
glorious appearing of the great God and
our Saviour Jesus Christ.

Titus 2:13

HOPE

Soft as the voice, as the voice of a
  Zephyr, breathing unheard,
Hope gently whispers, through the shadows,
  Her comforting word:
Wait till the darkness is over,
  Wait till the tempest is done,
Hope for the sunshine, hope for the morrow,
  After the storm has gone.

AUTHOR UNKNOWN

Do not look forward to the changes and chances of this life in fear; rather look to them with full hope that, as they arise, God, whose you are, will deliver you out of them. He is your Keeper. He has kept you hitherto. Do you but hold fast to His dear hand, and He will lead you safely through all things; and, when you cannot stand, He will bear you in His arms. Do not look forward to what may happen tomorrow. Our Father will either shield you from suffering, or He will give you strength to bear it.

SAINT FRANCIS DE SALES

True hope is swift and flies with swallow's wings;
Kings it makes gods, and meaner creatures kings.

WILLIAM SHAKESPEARE
Richard III

BEGIN AGAIN

Every day is a fresh beginning,
  Every morn is the world made new.
You who are weary of sorrow and sinning,
  Here is a beautiful hope for you,—
  A hope for me and a hope for you.

Every day is a fresh beginning;
  Listen, my soul, to the glad refrain,
And, spite of old sorrow and older sinning,
  And puzzles forecasted and possible pain,
  Take heart with the day, and begin again.
                              SUSAN COOLIDGE

Make us Thy mountaineers:
We would not linger on the lower slope,
Fill us afresh with hope, O God of Hope,
That undefeated we may climb the hill
As seeing Him who is invisible.
                        AMY CARMICHAEL
                        "The Last Defile"

Those are dead even for this life who hope
for no other.
          JOHANN WOLFGANG VON GOETHE

THE DAY—THE WAY

  Not for one single day
  Can I discern my way,
    But this I surely know—
  Who gives the day
  Will show the way,
    So I securely go.
          JOHN OXENHAM

  Stone walls do not a prison make,
    Nor iron bars a cage;
  Minds innocent and quiet take
    That for an hermitage:

If I have freedom in my love,
And in my soul am free,
Angels alone, that soar above,
Enjoy such liberty.
RICHARD LOVELACE
"To Althea From Prison"

My experience of men has neither disposed me to think worse of them nor indisposed me to serve them; not, in spite of failures which I lament, of errors which I now see and acknowledge, or of the present aspect of affairs, do I despair of the future. The truth is this: The march of Providence is so slow and our desires so impatient; the work of progress is so immense and our means of aiding it so feeble; the life of humanity is so long, that of the individual so brief, that we often see only the ebb of the advancing wave and are thus discouraged. It is history that teaches us to hope.

ROBERT E. LEE

I steer my bark with Hope ahead and
Fear astern.
THOMAS JEFFERSON

There are no rules of architecture for a castle in the clouds.
G. K. CHESTERTON

If you have built castles in the air,
Your work need not be lost—
that is where they should be.
Now put foundations under them.
HENRY DAVID THOREAU

God's gifts put man's best dreams to shame.
ELIZABETH BARRETT BROWNING

Ah, but a man's reach should exceed his grasp,
Or what's a heaven for?
ROBERT BROWNING
Andrea del Sarto

Lord, grant that I may always desire more
than I can accomplish.

MICHELANGELO

The vision has its own appointed hour,
it ripens, it will flower;
if it be long, then wait,
for it is sure, and it will not be late.

Habakkuk 2:3
(MOFFATT translation)

Hope is wishing for a thing to come true;
faith is believing that it will come true.

NORMAN VINCENT PEALE

If God shuts one door, He opens another.

IRISH PROVERB

Hope is the thing with feathers
That perches in the soul,
And sings the tune without the words,
And never stops at all,

And sweetest in the gale is heard;
And sore must be the storm
That could abash the little bird
That kept so many warm.

I've heard it in the chillest land,
And on the strangest sea;
Yet, never, in extremity,
It asked a crumb of me.

EMILY DICKINSON

Man is based on hope. He has no other
possession but hope.

THOMAS CARLYLE

Eternity is the divine treasure house, and
hope is the window, by means of which
mortals are permitted to see, as through a
glass darkly, the things which God is pre-
paring.

LORD MOUNTFORD

The daily work in narrow space is bound
Which each moment brings within our prison yard,
As one by one we circle round the guard
But skyward ever hearts and eyes we lift,
That wander far into God's realm of light,
That rise untrammeled as the bird so swift,
That bear to God our praises and our trust.

By a prisoner in a Nazi
concentration camp, 1940

Yesterday is already a dream
And tomorrow is only a vision,
But today, well-lived,
Makes every yesterday a dream
of happiness and
Every tomorrow a
vision of hope.

AUTHOR UNKNOWN

Hope springs eternal in the human breast:
Man never is, but always to be blest.

ALEXANDER POPE

The grand essentials to happiness in this
life are something to do, something to love,
and something to hope for.

JOSEPH ADDISON

Hope is the dream of a man awake.

MATTHEW PRIOR

And I said to the man who stood at the gate of the year:
"Give me a light, that I may tread safely into the unknown."
And he replied:
"Go out into the darkness and put your hand into the Hand of God.
That shall be to you better than light and safer than a known way."

M. LOUISE HASKINS

(These lines were quoted by King George VI
in a radio speech at the beginning of World War II.)

Lord Jesus, as I live in the hope of Your return, give me Your love and wisdom to reach out to others who need Your consolation. I rejoice in the wonder of Your love. Amen.

—*J. W. B.*

Beauty

In all ranks of life the human heart yearns for the beautiful; and the beautiful things that God makes are His gift to all alike.

—HARRIET BEECHER STOWE

It's beautiful!" These were the words that Lil Dickson spoke as she and her husband stood on the deck of the ship that had brought them from America to the island of Formosa. Jim had been assigned as a missionary to this land of twelve million people. Together they worked for many years, lessening suffering wherever possible. The beauty of the island belied the harrowing, tragic lives of so many of its inhabitants.

Barely five feet tall, the little woman with the indomitable spirit would hardly be called beautiful by the world's standards. For one thing her hair and dress were not fashionable—her features were not classic or striking. But Lillian Dickson's face shone with a beauty that came from within; it was the love of Christ that dominated this remarkable woman.

Lil's heart—her "mother's heart," she said—not only was filled with compassion, but compassion that had "wings." Seeing a need, she would immediately set out to do something about it, many times with great courage as she met opposition from the authorities. Miles of red tape were cut as "Typhoon Lil," with chin up and determination in her eyes, demanded action for the people she had come to love.

While visiting a leprosarium run by the government, Lil was horrified to see the vile conditions in which these people lived. Many were committing suicide. Bending over a young soldier who had tried, but failed, she whispered, "Why did you do it?" The youth, with bitterness in both his eyes and voice, told her it was because he had the terrible disease for which there was no cure and because he was in such a dreadful place. But most of all, it was because nobody cared.

"Somebody does care," Lil told him. "This will not always be a dreadful place. And some day there will be a cure."

She brought the official in charge of the United States aid distribution to see the leprosarium and $300 thousand was given. Beautiful new dormitories were built, and Lil helped to change the ugliness that surrounded the lepers' lives. Always she wanted people to be able to live in beauty.

Today there is a walkway to the church she had built for the lepers—they named it Lillian Walk. Part of it was once a swamp; now there is a fountain surrounded by enormous water lilies, and as the lepers make their way to church they are reminded of the beauty of God's Creation and the beautiful life of a lady they called *Mother*. Never repulsed by the sight of the lepers, Lil saw beyond their disfigurement to souls that still could shine with the light and beauty of Christ. Hers was not a pitying love but a love that was Christlike— able to reach out and change the ugliness of life, not only for a while but for eternity.

"How could anyone do all this for us?" were the incredulous words of a young boy when he first saw the lovely Boys Home she had built. Straight from prison, he experienced real love for the first time. Today, in addition to homes for young boys, there are orphanages, sanitariums, hospitals, maternity homes, and the list goes on and on. Lil Dickson, "Littlest Lady with the Biggest Heart," not only cared, but with God's strength and love, she set out to bring true beauty into the lives of thousands.

—*J. W. B.*

Lillian Dickson writes in *These My People:*

. . . We meet sordidness, ugliness and drabness not with the defense of hardening ourselves so that we cannot see or feel it, but by meeting it squarely, recognizing it, and then looking through it to the glory and the beauty that lie beyond and beneath it. A life that has not glory in it is not beautiful; a soul that has not vision is surely dead; but in almost every life, even of those who have never heard the Gospel, one can glimpse beauty, wistfulness, hunger for better things, if one looks well. It is called "second sight"—to see the souls of men, not just their clothes, to see "The Common Street" lit up with heaven's glory.

And yet, from sordid and from base,
Passion can lift a shining face . . .
And walking through a street at night
I saw a jail in soft moonlight;
And there, behind the chequered bars,
A still shape came to look at stars . . . .

CONRAD AIKEN

To those who hunger—"the Bread of
Life"—To those who thirst—"the Living
Water" . . . To those who come "to look
at stars"—the beauty of the message of
God, of love, peace through Christ, truth
and everlasting sureties . . . .

LILLIAN DICKSON
These My People

O Heavenly Father, who hast filled the world with beauty: Open, we
beseech thee, our eyes to behold thy gracious hand in all thy works, that
rejoicing in thy whole creation, we may learn to serve thee with glad-
ness; for the sake of him through whom all things were made, thy Son
Jesus Christ our Lord. *Amen.*

Book of Common Prayer (USA)

How beautiful upon the mountains are the
feet of him that bringeth good tidings, that
publisheth peace; that bringeth good tidings of good, that publisheth salvation;
that saith unto Zion, Thy God reigneth!

Isaiah 52:7

Malcolm Muggeridge writes of a time in Calcutta when he went to see
Mother Teresa off on a train:

When the train began to move and I walked
away, I felt as though I were leaving behind me all the beauty and all the joy of the
universe. Something of God's universal
love has rubbed off on Mother Teresa giv-

ing her homely features a shining quality.
She has lived so closely with her Lord that
the same enchantment clings about her that
sent the crowds chasing after Him in
Jerusalem and Galilee.

These are the things I prize
  And hold of dearest worth:
Light of the sapphire skies,
Peace of the silent hills,
Shelter of the forest, comfort of the grass,
Music of birds, murmur of little rills,
Shadows of clouds that swiftly pass,
    And, after showers,
    The smell of flowers
And of the good brown earth—
And best of all, along the way, friendship and mirth.
                                                    HENRY VAN DYKE

There is no beautifier of complexion, or
form, or behavior, like the wish to scatter
joy and not pain around us.
                                                    RALPH WALDO EMERSON

She walks in beauty like the night
  Of cloudless climes and starry skies;
And all that's best of dark and bright
  Meet in her aspect and her eyes:
Thus mellow'd to that tender light
  Which heaven to gaudy day denies.
                                                    LORD BYRON

After all, it is the divinity within that
makes the divinity without; and I have
been more fascinated by a woman of talent
and intelligence, though deficient in personal charms, than I have been by the most
regular beauty.
                                                    WASHINGTON IRVING

The beautiful is a phenomenon which is
never apparent of itself, but is reflected in a
thousand different works of the creator.

JOHANN WOLFGANG VON GOETHE

Truth is beautiful.

RALPH WALDO EMERSON

A thing of beauty is a joy forever:
Its loveliness increases; it will never
Pass into nothingness; but still will keep
A bower quiet for us, and a sleep
Full of sweet dreams, and health, and quiet breathing.

JOHN KEATS

To see a World in a grain of sand,
    And a Heaven in a wild flower,
Hold Infinity in the palm of your hand,
    And Eternity in an hour.

WILLIAM BLAKE

Beauty is a gift of God.

ARISTOTLE

One thing have I desired of the Lord, that
will I seek after; that I may dwell in the
house of the Lord all the days of my life, to
behold the beauty of the Lord . . . .

Psalms 27:4

*Everywhere there is a touch of Your beauty, Almighty God. Thank
You for the reminders of Your love and care. As I see a tree begin to
bud in spring, I am reminded that out of seeming barrenness there
comes the promise of life. Through Your Son I shall know one day
the beauty of heaven for all eternity. In His name I pray, amen.*

—J. W. B.

Home

Home that our feet may leave,
but not our hearts.
—AUTHOR UNKNOWN

The charming colonial house on King Street in Northampton, Massachusetts, was more than a house—it was a warm, loving, but often tempestuous home. To many a traveler, the sight of the latchstring hanging outside the front door meant a welcome and endearing hospitality. One of America's greatest preachers and theologians, the Reverend Jonathan Edwards and his wife, Sarah, together with their eleven children, brought life and love to the bricks and mortar which were used in the construction of their home.

Jonathan Edwards was a loving, impassioned, unpredictable, and trying man, often given to depression. Sarah loved him in a very wonderful way. She knew his shortcomings, but realized the genius that lay behind his moods. Because of his work as a minister, there was little money, but Sarah worked to make her home attractive; the children were well dressed and fed and she was always well groomed. Each child was made to feel important in carrying out the many daily tasks. Without their doing their part, it would have been impossible to keep the house in any kind of order.

Sarah was to find that her husband had many annoying traits. One of these was his extremely early rising. Even before the farmers would awaken to milk the cows, he would have been up some time, expecting the whole household to join him in Bible reading and prayers by candlelight. Sarah adjusted to his hours. Jonathan was hardly ever on time for meals and even when he did join the family, he would suddenly get up and return to his studies and writing. However, each night he gave one hour of completely undivided attention to his children; listening to their needs and praying with them. Perhaps the greatest memory they had of their parents was to see the love and respect that their father and mother had for each other. A family could weather any storm if real love was the cornerstone of the home.

But theirs was a completely natural family. Many fights broke out among the children, and Sarah always dealt with these small crises with love and firm discipline. She had the gift of never making a child feel unworthy or rejected, but encouraged their natural abilities and talents. With all her responsibilities in the home, she still found time to sit down over a cup of tea and listen to another person's troubles.

No matter how loving a person is, sometimes he can overextend himself, and this happened to Sarah. She suddenly found herself in the depths of depression and suffered many dark days, on the verge of a complete breakdown. One day she began to talk to Jonathan about her innermost feelings—her frustrations. As the two talked, they realized Sarah had been trying to *earn* God's love and had done so many things in her own strength, which had failed her. Also, she always wanted to be popular with everyone. As they talked and prayed, an awakening came of God's unconditional love for her—just as she was—and from then on, life became a joy, instead of one that was based on duty.

Jonathan Edwards became president of the College of New Jersey, later named Princeton, but died shortly afterwards from an inoculation against smallpox. Sarah was in the midst of packing so that she could join him when a letter arrived telling of the tragedy. His last words were of her:

> Give my love to my dear wife, and tell her
> that the uncommon union which has so
> long subsisted between us has been of such
> a nature as I trust is spiritual and therefore
> will continue forever.

History shows that the heritage of this "uncommon union" between Jonathan and Sarah Edwards in succeeding generations was to be responsible for:

- A vice-president of the United States
- Governors of three states
- Controller of the United States Treasury
- Mayors of three cities
- Eighty in public office
- Thirteen college presidents
- One hundred lawyers
- Sixty-five professors
- Dean of a prominent law school
- Thirty judges
- Sixty-six physicians
- Dean of a medical school

—J. W. B.

The Christian home is the Master's work-
shop where the processes of character
molding are silently, lovingly, faithfully,
and successfully carried on.

LORD HOUGHTON

Lord, behold our family here assembled. We thank Thee for this place
in which we dwell; for the love that unites us; for the peace accorded us
this day; for the hope with which we expect the morrow; for the health,
the work, the food, and the bright skies that make our lives delightful;
for our friends in all parts of the earth, and our friendly helpers in this
foreign isle . . . .

Give us courage, gaiety, and the quiet mind. Spare to us our friends,
soften to us our enemies. Bless us, if it may be, in all our innocent
endeavors. If it may not, give us the strength to encounter that which is
to come, that we be brave in peril, constant in tribulation, temperate in
wrath, and in all changes of fortune and down to the gates of death, loyal
and loving one to another. *Amen.*

ROBERT LOUIS STEVENSON

Sweet is the smile of home; the mutual look
When hearts are of each other sure.

JOHN KEBLE

But what on earth is half so dear—
So longed for—
As the hearth of home?

EMILY BRONTË

There is beauty in homely things which many
        people have never seen . . .
Sunlight through a jar of beach-plum jelly;
    A rainbow in soapsuds in dishwater;
An egg yolk in a blue bowl;
    White ruffled curtains sifting moonlight;

The color of cranberry glass;
   A little cottage with blue shutters;
Crimson roses in an old stone crock;
   The smell of newly baked bread;
Candlelight on old brass;
   The soft brown of a cocker's eyes.
                PETER MARSHALL
                Mr. Jones, Meet the Master

Christ is the Head of this house,
The unseen Guest at every meal,
The silent Listener to every conversation.
                AUTHOR UNKNOWN

The first essential for a man's being a good citizen is his possession of the home virtues, based on recognition of the great underlying laws of religion and morality. No piled up wealth, no splendor of material growth, no brilliance of artistic development, will permanently avail any people unless its home life is healthy.
                THEODORE ROOSEVELT

Home is where the heart is.
                PLINY

He is happiest, be he king or peasant, who
finds his peace in his home.
                JOHANN WOLFGANG VON GOETHE

Robert Rainy, the Scottish churchman, had been facing tremendous criticism and controversy. His friends were amazed at how well he seemed able to bear it. "Ah, but then, you see," said Rainy, "I'm very happy at home."

To be happy at home is the ultimate result
of all ambition.
                SAMUEL JOHNSON

If there is righteousness in the heart,
   there will be beauty in the character.
If there be beauty in the character,
   there will be harmony in the home.

If there is harmony in the home,
   there will be order in the nation.
When there is order in the nation,
   there will be peace in the world.
AUTHOR UNKNOWN

In every house should be a window toward
the sky.
AUTHOR UNKNOWN

A good laugh is sunshine in a house.
WILLIAM MAKEPEACE THACKERAY

Go where he will, the wise man is at home,
His hearth the earth—his hall the azure dome;
Where his clear spirit leads him, there's his road,
By God's own light illumined and foreshadowed.
RALPH WALDO EMERSON

The many make the household, but only
one the home.
JAMES RUSSELL LOWELL

Every house where love abides and friendship is a guest, is surely home, and home,
sweet home; for there the heart can rest.
HENRY VAN DYKE

There is no spectacle on earth more appeal-
ing than that of a beautiful woman in the
act of cooking dinner for someone she
loves.
THOMAS WOLFE
The Web and the Rock

There is beauty all around
When there's love at home;
There is joy in every sound
When there's love at home.

Peace and plenty here abide,
Smiling sweet on every side;
Time doth softly, sweetly glide
When there's love at home.

AUTHOR UNKNOWN

Peace and rest at length have come,
  All the day's long toil is past,
And each heart is whispering, "Home,
  Home at last."

THOMAS HOOD

There is no place more delightful than home.

CICERO

So long as there are homes to which men turn
At close of day;
So long as there are homes where children are,
Where women stay—
If love and loyalty and faith be found
Across those sills—
A stricken nation can recover from
Its gravest ills.

So long as there are homes where fires burn
And there is bread;
So long as there are homes where lamps are lit
And prayers are said;
Although people falter through the dark—
And nations grope—
With God himself back of these little homes—
We have sure hope.

GRACE NOLL CROWELL

A happy family is but an earlier heaven.

JOHN BOWRING

For this cause shall a man leave his father
and mother, and cleave to his wife;

And they twain shall be one flesh: so then
they are no more twain, but one flesh.

What therefore God hath joined together,
let not man put asunder.

Mark 10:7–9

PSALM FOR A GOOD MARRIAGE

Lord God of Earth and Sky, whose hand hath harnessed the wind
and the rain, whose ear hath marked the pounding of the surf
and the small night stir of crickets in the grass;

Bless them this day!

Make Thy light to shine upon their faces as they cross the threshold
of this wedded life;

Let their souls be the wide windows to the sun and their minds
open to the light of mutual understanding;

Let contentment be as a roof over their heads and humility as a
carpet for their feet;

Give them love's tenderness for their days of sorrow and love's
pride for their days of joy;

Let the voices of children ring sweetly on their ears and the faces of
children glow round their hearth-fire;

Let not the evil bird of envy darken their ways or the poisonous
fangs of greed sting their hands;

Give them high hearts;

Let beauty dwell with them—
In the sheen of copper pans and the cool folding of linen,

In the shining surface of china and tinkle of glass; give them, O
Lord, these blessings of the simple life;

Make theirs in truth a good marriage—

For Ever and Ever.

AUTHOR UNKNOWN

WHERE THERE IS LOVE

Where there is love the heart is light,
Where there is love the day is bright,
Where there is love there is a song
To help when things are going wrong . . .
Where there is love there is a smile
To make all things seem more worthwhile,
Where there is love there's quiet peace,
A tranquil place where turmoils cease—
Love changes darkness into light
And makes the heart take "wingless flight" . . .
Oh, blest are they who walk in love,
They also walk with God above—
And when you walk with God each day
And kneel together when you pray,
Your marriage will be truly blest
And God will be your daily "GUEST"—
And love that once seemed yours alone,
God gently blends into HIS OWN.

HELEN STEINER RICE

When Queen Elizabeth was married to
Prince Philip in Westminster Abbey, the
Archbishop of Canterbury said to them:
"The ever-living Christ is here to bless
you. The nearer you keep to Him, the
nearer you will be to one another."

Let me not to the marriage of true minds
Admit impediments. Love is not love
Which alters when it alteration finds,
Or bends with the remover to remove:
O, no! it is an ever-fixed mark,
That looks on tempests and is never shaken;
It is the star to every wand'ring bark,

Whose worth's unknown, although his height be taken.
Love's not Time's fool, though rosy lips and cheeks
Within his bending sickle's compass come;
Love alters not with his brief hours and weeks,
But bears it out even to the edge of doom:—
　　　If this be error and upon me proved,
　　　I never writ, nor no man ever loved.

WILLIAM SHAKESPEARE
Sonnets

Paul says, "The love of Christ constrains us." As I see it, there is no way for a husband to demand submission on the part of his wife without violating the command of God for him to be loving. Let the love of Christ in him have that constraining effect on a wife and he may discover that she is no longer rebellious or fearful about the idea of submitting to that kind of leadership in the home.

"You wives must submit to your husband's leadership in the same way you submit to the Lord." There is no suggestion here that a woman submits to a man's leadership because he is superior or she is inferior. As I see it, the only possible reason she should submit to his leadership is because of the awful responsibilities he has in the eyes of God. When we elect a government official to a position of responsibility, we must confer on him the necessary authority to fulfill the responsibility. The same thing is true in the home. It is only because of the responsibility that the man must have the authority. However, since he cannot compel the woman to give him that authority, the only way he will ever get it is for her to confer that authority on him. The reason she should confer that authority on him is that he bears the responsibility that God has laid on his shoulders.

LANE ADAMS

The story is related—probably true—that one day a very angry Prince Albert locked himself in his room. An equally angry Queen Victoria knocked imperiously on the door to be admitted.

"Who is there?" asked Albert.

"The Queen of England," was the haughty reply.

Nothing.

She knocked again—and again—again. He asked the same question; she gave the same answer.

Another silence. Then came a gentle knock.

"Who is there?" Albert asked once again.

Softly. "Your wife, Albert."

And the Prince opened the door.

Getting married or raising children doesn't completely fulfil a woman. Having a career does not produce peace. Neither prestige nor power brings purpose. Money can't make a happy atmosphere at the breakfast table. Education can't take away the lump in your throat or the ache in your heart. Nothing that man can do can prevent sickness, or disappointment, or death.

What is the purpose of it all? I believe a woman is just spinning her wheels until she is fulfilled by the Ultimate, God Himself. He is the only One who can get it all together. He is the only One who can keep it there. He is the only One who can make you complete—*total*. He is the only One who can give you a good attitude all the time. And best of all, He offers to you the possibility of a life of no regrets.

His name: Jesus of Nazareth, the God-Man.

MARABEL MORGAN
Total Joy

As I went up the White House steps, Edith came to meet me at the door, and I suddenly realized that, after all, no matter what the outcome of the election was, my happiness was assured—that even though my ambition to have the seal of approval put upon my administration might not be gratified, my happiness was assured—for my life with Edith and my children constitutes my happiness.

THEODORE ROOSEVELT

An ideal wife is any woman who has an ideal husband.

BOOTH TARKINGTON

A HUSBAND TO A WIFE

Trusty, dusky, vivid, true,
With eyes of gold and bramble-dew,
Steel true and blade-straight,
The great artificer
Made my mate.

Honour, anger, valour, fire;
A love that life could never tire,
Death quench or evil stir,
The mighty Master
Gave to her.

Teacher, tender, comrade, wife,
    A fellow-farer true through life,
    Heart-whole and soul-free,
The august Father
Gave to me.

ROBERT LOUIS STEVENSON

To turn to her in stress and storm was like going into a sheltered haven where waters are at rest. When I was weary and worn, buffeted, and discouraged, thinking only of giving up the thankless strife, . . . my lady would heal and soothe me with her cheery faith and conviction, and send me forth to smite and be smitten.

RAMSAY MAC DONALD
A tribute to his wife

God transforms us, our marriage, and our children only after we really believe Him! Paul, in his letter to the Thessalonians, said, "And we will never stop thanking God for this: that when we preached to you, you didn't think of the words we spoke as being just our own, but you accepted what we said as the very Word of God—which, of course, it was—and it changed your lives when you believed it" (1 Thessalonians 2:13). The key words in that verse are: "when you believed it."

By believing God's Word and really practicing it in daily living, the changes and the exchanges are truly miraculous. Husband and wife, mother and daughter, father and son, even community and job relations are sharply altered and changed by believing.

JOYCE LANDORF
His Stubborn Love

LUCY ANN TUCKER—DIED 1812

was admired, respected and beloved. She lived an
ornament of the society in which she moved. The kind
neighbor and friend, the charm of her household, the
faithful wife, the devoted mother, the pure Christian.

In her life and character were happily blended gentleness and firmness, affability and dignity. She died
lamented as living she was beloved by all classes of
the community.

> Epitaph on a tombstone in the
> churchyard at Williamsburg, Va.

Who can find a virtuous woman? for her price is far above
rubies . . . .
Strength and honour are her clothing; and she shall rejoice in time to
come.
She openeth her mouth with wisdom; and in her tongue is the law of
kindness.
She looketh well to the ways of her household, and eateth not the
bread of idleness.
Her children arise up, and call her blessed; her husband also, and he
praiseth her.
Many daughters have done virtuously, but thou excellest them all.
Favour is deceitful, and beauty is vain: but a woman that feareth the
Lord, she shall be praised.
Give her of the fruit of her hands; and let her own works praise her in
the gates.

> Proverbs 31:10, 25–31

TRIBUTE TO A MOTHER

Faith that withstood the shocks of toil and time;
    Hope that defied despair;
    Patience that conquered care;
And loyalty, whose courage was sublime;
The great deep heart that was a home for all—
    Just, eloquent, and strong
    In protest against wrong;

Wide charity, that knew no sin, no fall;
The Spartan spirit that made life so grand,
   Mating poor daily needs
   With high, heroic deeds,
That wrested happiness from Fate's hard hand.
                                    LOUISA MAY ALCOTT

   All that I am or hope to be, I owe to my
   angel mother.
                                    ABRAHAM LINCOLN

   All that I am my mother made me.
                                    JOHN QUINCY ADAMS

Being a mother is what makes a real life for a woman, not applause,
your picture in the paper, the roses and the telegrams you get on open-
ing night. A great many people who think of themselves as poor have
that richness in their lives.
   You are a person of the greatest importance when you are a mother of
a family. Just do your job right and your kids will love you. And for that
love of theirs there is no satisfying substitute.
                                    ETHEL WATERS
                                    His Eye Is on the Sparrow

   Mothers' arms are made of tenderness, and
   sweet sleep blesses the child who lies
   therein.
                                    VICTOR HUGO

For when you looked into my mother's eyes,
   you knew, as if He had told you,
Why God sent her into the world—
it was to open the minds of all who looked,
   to beautiful thoughts.
                                    SIR JAMES M. BARRIE

Youth fades; love droops; the leaves
   of friendship fall:
A mother's secret love outlives them all.
                                    OLIVER WENDELL HOLMES

THE MOTHER'S PRAYER

Lord, give me this soul!
I have waked for it when I should have slept,
I have yearned over it, and I have wept,
Till in my own the thought of it held sway
    All through the night and day.

Lord, give me this soul!
If I might only lift its broken strands,
To lay them gently in Thy loving hands—
If I might know it had found peace in Thee,
    What rest, what peace to me!

Thou wilt give me this soul!
Else why the joy, the grief, the doubt, the pain
The thought perpetual, the one refrain,
The ceaseless longing that upon Thy breast
The tempest-tossed may rest?
    Dear Lord, give me this soul!
                    AUTHOR UNKNOWN

Where there is a mother in the house, mat-
ters speed well.
                    AMOS BRONSON ALCOTT

There is an enduring tenderness in the love of a mother to a son that
transcends all other affections of the heart. It is neither to be chilled by
selfishness, nor daunted by danger, nor weakened by worthlessness,
nor stifled by ingratitude. She will sacrifice every comfort to his con-
venience; she will surrender every pleasure to his enjoyment; she will
glory in his fame and exult in his prosperity; and if adversity overtake
him, he will be the dearer to her by misfortune; and if disgrace settle
upon his name, she will still love and cherish him; and if all the world
beside cast him off, she will be all the world to him.
                    WASHINGTON IRVING

Mother's love grows by giving.
                    CHARLES LAMB

PORTRAITS

As a portrait is unconscious
    Of the master artist's touch.
Unaware of growing beauty,
    Unaware of changing much
So you have not guessed His working
    In your life throughout each year,
Have not guessed the growing beauty,
    Have not sensed it, mother dear.
We have seen and marveled greatly
    At the Master artist's skill,
Marveled at the lovely picture
    Daily growing lovelier still
Watched His brush strokes change each
    Feature to a likeness of His face,
Till in you we see the Master,
    Feel His presence glimpse His grace.
May the fragrance of His presence
    Made through you grow doubly sweet,
Till your years on earth are ended
    And the portrait is complete.

RUTH BELL GRAHAM

The mother's heart is the child's schoolroom.

HENRY WARD BEECHER

The mother of Saint Augustine prayed constantly for her son to give his life to Christ. He had strayed far from all her teachings and she was very depressed as she discussed this with her bishop. "The child of so many prayers can never be lost," he told her.

Later, when Saint Augustine was converted he said, "If I am Thy child, O God, it is because Thou didst give me such a mother."

Honor thy father and thy mother: that thy
days may be long upon the land which the
Lord thy God giveth thee.

Exodus 20:12

By profession I am a soldier and take pride in that fact. But I am prouder, infinitely prouder, to be a father. A soldier destroys in order to build. The father only builds, never destroys. The one has the potentialities of death; the other embodies creation and life. And while the hordes of death are mighty, the battles of life are mightier still. My hope is that my son, when I am gone, will remember me not from the battle, but in the home, repeating with him one simple daily prayer, "Our Father which art in heaven."

GENERAL DOUGLAS MAC ARTHUR

THE GENERAL'S PRAYER

Build me a son, O Lord, who will be strong enough to know when he is weak, and brave enough to face himself when he is afraid; one who will be proud and unbending in honest defeat, and humble and gentle in victory.

Build me a son whose wishbone will not be where his backbone should be; a son who will know Thee and that to know himself is the foundation stone of knowledge.

Lead him, I pray, not in the path of ease and comfort, but under the stress and spur of difficulties and challenge. Here let him learn to stand up in the storm; here let him learn compassion for those who fail.

Build me a son whose heart will be clear, whose goal will be high; a son who will master himself before he seeks to master other men; one who will learn to laugh, yet never forget how to weep; one who will reach into the future, yet never forget the past.

And after all these things are his, add, I pray, enough of a sense of humor, so that he may always be serious, yet never take himself too seriously. Give him humility, so that he may always remember the simplicity of true greatness, the open mind of true wisdom, the meekness of true strength.

Then I, his father, will dare to whisper, "I have not lived in vain."

GENERAL DOUGLAS MAC ARTHUR

Blessed is he who is given the ability to discern between needs and wants and the wisdom to choose wisely, for he and his family will reap the rewards of prudence.

Blessed is he whose feet leave the soiled problems of his workday at the doormat of our Lord, for he will discover room in his heart to listen to the needs of others.

Blessed is he who dries the dishes of despair with the towel of tenderness, for he will find no lack of comfort from Him who loves us all.

Blessed is he who foregoes the round of golf to become companion to his children, for a legacy of memories is bequeathed in these happy hours.

Blessed is he who trims the hedge of misunderstanding between himself and his neighbor, for the blossom of friendship has a sweet and lasting fragrance.

Blessed is he who mends the toys of disillusionment with the permanent bond of love, for he mirrors the handiwork of God who hath remade our damaged frame.

Blessed is he whose home is built upon the Word of God, for his roof will be shingled with happiness and all who pass by will see the goodness of the Lord.

RICKS L. FALK
Decision magazine

He teaches patience—by being gentle and understanding over and over.

He teaches honesty—by keeping his promises to his family even when it costs.

He teaches courage—by living unafraid, with faith, in all circumstances.

He teaches justice—by being fair and dealing equally with everyone.

Every father can teach Christian principles.

He teaches kindness—by being thoughtful and gracious even at home.

AUTHOR UNKNOWN

One day a father was talking to a friend about his son, who had caused great heartache. The friend said: "If he were my son, I would kick him out." The father thought for a moment, then said, "Yes, if he were your son, so would I. But he is not your son, he is mine and I can't do it."

Dear Ann Landers:

I am a girl 18 years old and living at home with my father. One hears so much about the generation gap these days, but it doesn't exist in our family.

Every day my father tells me, "I trust you. I respect you. I believe in you. I love you." He doesn't actually speak the words, but the message comes across loud and clear. It's the look in his eyes. The way he just assumes I am doing the right thing.

It all adds up to confidence and faith. I'd rather die than let him down.

YOUR DAILY READER IN MICHIGAN

Dear Reader:

Your letter could be a sermon for parents everywhere. I've said it before, but thanks for providing me with an opportunity to say it again.

Children have a strange way of living up to your high opinion of them. And the reverse is true. If you keep telling a child he's no good—he'll prove you are right.

ANN LANDERS

Wisdom leads us back to childhood. Except
ye become as little children . . . .

BLAISE PASCAL

I love little children and it is not a slight
thing when they, who are fresh from God,
love us.

CHARLES DICKENS

A CHILD'S OFFERING

The wise may bring their learning,
   The rich may bring their wealth,
And some may bring their greatness,
   And some bring strength and health;
We, too, would bring our treasures
   To offer to the King;
We have no wealth or learning:
   What shall we children bring?

We'll bring Him hearts that love Him;
　　We'll bring Him thankful praise,
And young souls meekly striving
　　To walk in holy ways:
And these shall be the treasures
　　We offer to the King,
And these are gifts that even
　　The poorest child may bring.

The Book of Praise
for Children, 1881

I believe *the* most valuable contribution a parent can make to his child is to instill in him a genuine faith in God. What greater ego satisfaction could there be than knowing that the Creator of the Universe is acquainted with me, personally? That He values me more than the possessions of the entire world; that He understands my fears and my anxieties; that He reaches out to me in immeasurable love when no one else cares; that His only Son actually gave His life for me; that He can turn my liabilities into assets and my emptiness into fullness; that a better life follows this one, where the present handicaps and inadequacies will all be eliminated—where earthly pain and suffering will be no more than a dim memory! What a beautiful philosophy with which to "clothe" your tender child. What a fantastic message of hope and encouragement for the broken teen-ager who has been crushed by life's circumstances. This is self-esteem at its richest, not dependent on the whims of birth or social judgment, or the cult of the superchild, but on divine decree. If this be the opiate of the people, as Karl Marx said, then I have staked my entire life on the validity of its promise!

DR. JAMES DOBSON
Hide or Seek

God makes the world all over again
whenever a little child is born.

JEAN PAUL RICHTER

I prayed for greater joy in my salvation,
A selfish prayer I finally came to know,
For the greatest joy while living comes to me
　　when I am giving,
Giving children bread of life and watching them
　　grow.

And my greatest joy is knowing that my children
    walk in truth,
And that they are giving You, Lord, of their fire
    and strength of youth.

Yes, I found that the joy of my salvation,
Is knowing that my children walk in truth.

JOHNNY CASH

MY SON

I saw you for the first time today. The nurse held you up so that I could get a good look at you through the nursery window. There wasn't much of you that I could see, but I felt very proud. You were my son!

I was proud and thankful too—thankful to God for you, thankful that you were well and strong, with your tiny body in proper working order. Your mother and I had prayed that it might be so. And seeing you as you were today was the answer to our prayers.

And there were other things we had prayed about, things we shall continue to pray about as you grow up. That our words and our lives may lead you to know the Saviour that we know, the Lord Jesus Christ. That you may not only belong to us, but to Him. That Christ may be Lord of your life. For we know of nothing better than a life in Christ, and we wish the best for you.

AUTHOR UNKNOWN

Could I climb to the highest place in Athens, I would lift my voice and proclaim: "Fellow citizens, why do you turn and scrape every stone to gather wealth, and take so little care of your children to whom one day you must relinquish it all?"

SOCRATES

Let parents bequeath to their children not
riches, but the spirit of reverence.

PLATO

O Lord, make all the bad people good, and
all the good people nice.

A Little Girl's Prayer

You may give them your love but not your thoughts,
For they have their own thoughts.
You may house their bodies but not their souls,
For their souls dwell in the house of tomorrow,
     which you cannot visit, not even in your dreams.
You may strive to be like them, but seek not to
     make them like you.
For life goes not backward nor tarries with yesterday.
You are the bows from which your children as living
     arrows are sent forth.

KAHLIL GIBRAN
The Prophet

What gift has Providence bestowed on man
that is so dear to him as his children?

CICERO

From the services in which I joined as a child I have taken with me into life a feeling for what is solemn, and a need for quiet self-recollection, without which I cannot realize the meaning of my life. I cannot, therefore, support the opinion of those who would not let children take part in grown-up people's services till they to some extent understand them. The important thing is not that they shall understand but that they shall feel something of what is serious and solemn. The fact that a child sees his elders full of devotion, and has to feel something of devotion himself, that is what gives the service its meaning for him.

ALBERT SCHWEITZER

God says children must be taught obedience and discipline. Anything worthwhile requires effort on the parents' part. Children need the security of parental authority as described in the Bible—authority administered with patience and love.

Today's young generation has grown up for the most part with too little loving discipline. These young people often say their parents hate them. The Bible would bear the kids out, for it says the father who doesn't chasten his son, hates his son (Proverbs 13:24). Children somehow know this. They know it takes more love and hard work to discipline them.

ANITA BRYANT
Bless This House

You are the trip I did not take;
You are the pearls I cannot buy;
You are my blue Italian lake;
You are my piece of foreign sky.

ANNE CAMPBELL
"To My Child"

Children are the anchors that hold a mother
to life.

SOPHOCLES

THE CHOIR BOY

In his white surplice there he stands,
A hymnal in his boyish hands;
The morning sun upon his hair
Suggests a halo circling there.

His voice as sweet and fresh to hear
As feathered songbird singing clear;
His eyes as innocent and blue
As skies with heaven shining through.

Is this the boy who all the week
Brought worried lines to father's cheek?
Is this the mischievous small lad
Whom teacher found so very bad?

It cannot be! but mother, who
Serenely listens from her pew,
Feels truly what the others miss—
At heart he always is like this!

ANNE CAMPBELL

The great man is he who does not lose his
child's heart.

MENCIUS

Last night my little boy confessed to me
Some childish wrong;
And kneeling at my knee,
He prayed with tears—
"Dear God, make me a man
Like Daddy—wise and strong;
I know You can."

Then while he slept
I knelt beside his bed,
Confessed my sins,
And prayed with low-bowed head—
"O God, make me a child
Like my child here—
Pure, guileless,
Trusting Thee with faith sincere."

ANDREW GILLIES

I took a piece of plastic clay
And idly fashioned it one day.
And as my fingers pressed it, still
It moved and yielded to my will.

I came again when days were past:
The bit of clay was hard at last.
The form I gave it still it bore,
And I could fashion it no more!

I took a piece of living clay,
And gently pressed it day by day,
And moulded with my power and art
A young child's soft and yielding heart.

I came again when years had gone:
It was a man I looked upon.
He still that early impress bore,
And I could fashion it no more!

AUTHOR UNKNOWN

Life is a flame that is always burning itself
out, but it catches fire again every time a
child is born.

BERNARD SHAW

We need love's tender lessons taught
    As only weakness can;
God hath his small interpreters;
    The child must teach the man.
                    JOHN GREENLEAF WHITTIER

SIXTEEN

When she was small, I tried to teach her faith—
    I always held her hand to cross the street,
And so she learned to trust. But now, dear Lord,
    She needs Your love to guide her eager feet.

I hoped to make her brave, and when she cried
    From little hurts, I sent her back to play.
Lord, give her courage for a shield against
    The deeper pain that life will bring, I pray.

I told her that the world has need
    Of tenderness and song, Oh, more than anything.
God, I have set the words upon her lips,
    But only You can teach her heart to sing.
                    VIOLA DOWNEN

WHY GOD MADE LITTLE GIRLS

God made the world with the towering trees
Majestic mountains and restless seas
Then paused and said, "It needs one more thing—
Someone to laugh and dance and sing—
To walk in the woods and gather flowers—
To commune with nature in quiet hours";
So God made little girls
With laughing eyes and bouncing curls—
With joyful hearts and infectious smiles—
Enchanting ways and feminine wiles—
And when He completed the task He'd begun,
He was pleased and proud of the job He'd done;
For the world, when seen through a little girl's eyes
Greatly resembles Paradise.
                    AUTHOR UNKNOWN

IF

If you can keep your head when all about you
    Are losing theirs and blaming it on you;
If you can trust yourself when all men doubt you,
    But make allowance for their doubting too;
If you can wait and not be tired by waiting,
    Or being lied about, don't deal in lies,
Or being hated don't give way to hating,
    And yet don't look too good, nor talk too wise;

If you can talk with crowds and keep your virtue,
    Or walk with Kings—nor lose the common touch;
If neither foes nor loving friends can hurt you;
    If all men count with you, but none too much;
If you can fill the unforgiving minute
    With sixty seconds' worth of distance run—
Yours is the Earth and everything that's in it,
    And—which is more—you'll be a Man, my son!

RUDYARD KIPLING

Heavenly Father, how grateful I am for the joy of my home. For the times it is filled with loved ones' voices and for the days of solitude, when Your love and care still surround me, I thank You, Lord. Even though our steps may lead us far from this place, may our hearts remember the gift You have given us in providing an earthly home. In Jesus' name, amen.

—J. W. B.

Age and Youth

Winter is on my head, but eternal spring is in
my heart.

—VICTOR HUGO

Some people dread the thought of losing their youth and are always searching
for the secret that will keep them young. Ethel Waters found that secret, for the
key is not a transitory element but an eternal one. She found Jesus Christ and
together they conquered the fear of growing old.

Ethel Waters overcame many things in her extraordinary life. Being an inse-
cure, illegitimate child in the poverty-stricken ghettos of Chester, Pennsylvania, she experienced the tremendous trauma of feeling unloved and the prejudice of being black. She found "love" as she had never known before from
audiences who adored her for her talent when she emerged as an incredible
performer, not only of song, but as an actress of rare quality. But the love she
experienced over the footlights eluded her in her own private life until one day
she discovered how much Jesus loved her.

In *The Member of the Wedding*, a play on Broadway in which she received rave
reviews, she sang a song that expressed her childlike belief—"His eye is on the
sparrow, and I know He watches me." As God's "sparrow" aged, one could see
His beauty exemplified in Ethel Waters—the glow of His love in her eyes or in
her voice as she sang or talked about Him. Her great concern was that all the
"sparrows" she met would know about the same Lord who cared for all of them.

In an excerpt from her book *To Me It's Wonderful*, Ethel talked about the joy
she knew:

> I'm into my old age now, but I don't have
> anything special to say to older people any
> more than I have to young. People are
> people. The young have the handicap of no

experience. The old have the handicap of infirmity, of weakened bodies, and sometimes they're confused in their minds. So are the young. What keeps me steady in my old age is what I've already told—closeness to Jesus. This will keep the young steady too. He wants to be close to anyone who will let Him. No matter their age. To me it's wonderful!

Late in my life I bared myself to Him. He crumbled me and put me back together *His way.* The way I was meant to be in the first place. Everything I held dear or held *to* had to be broken, but as bad as brokenness sounds to people outside of Christ, it isn't bad. It's *essential.* None of what He did in any way lessened me as a human being. It lessened my strain inside. It lessened the burden of running my own life without help. But I'm still the same Ethel in all the ways that were God's ways to begin with. I still have a knocked-out sense of humor. God's humor is terrific! I don't get lonely no more, because Jesus is with me, but I understand the person who is lonely. Way back when I had so much of what the world counts necessary, I was lonely. Now that I have so little, loneliness is *out* because I have so much to be thankful for, and when you're thankful, you can't be lonely, *or* be sorry for yourself.

—*J. W. B.*

I have been young, and now am old; yet have I not seen the righteous forsaken . . . .

Psalms 37:25

Nature gives to every time and season
some beauties of its own; and from morning to night, as from the cradle to the grave,
is but a succession of changes so gentle and
easy that we can scarcely mark their progress.

CHARLES DICKENS

Grow old along with me!
The best is yet to be,
The last of life, for which the first was made:
Our times are in His hand
Who saith 'A whole I planned,
Youth shows but half; trust God: see all,
nor be afraid!''

ROBERT BROWNING
Rabbi Ben Ezra

As for old age, embrace and love it. It
abounds with pleasure if you know how to
use it. The gradually declining years are
among the sweetest in a man's life; and I
maintain that even when they have
reached the extreme limit, they have their
pleasure still.

SENECA

Youth is not a time of life—it is a state of mind. It is not a matter of red
cheeks, red lips, and supple knees. It is a temper of the will, a quality of
the imagination, a vigor of the emotions; it is a freshness of the deep
springs of life. Youth means a temperamental predominance of courage
over timidity, of the appetite for adventure over a life of ease. This often
exists in a man of fifty more than in a boy of twenty. Nobody grows old
by merely living a number of years; people grow old by deserting their
ideals.

SAMUEL ULLMAN

No wise man ever wished to be younger.

JONATHAN SWIFT

COMMUNION

I thank Thee, Lord, for planting in my heart
These needs—yea these desires:
Arbutus, pale and lovely with the glow
Of flushing sunrise underneath the snow;
The freshening feel of wind upon my face,
The movement of bare branches, full of grace;
The sight of children playing in the sun,
The satisfaction of a task well done.

I trust that I shall never grow too old
To thrill with glad surprise when I behold
The simple things of beauty close to me,
A rainbow in the sky, a dogwood tree;
The incense of the pines, the sharp outline
Of frosty, silver-plated firs that shine
Gray 'gainst the winter sky o'erhead, below,
The pure and seamless garment of the snow.

IONE W. LYALL
After the Rain

Wrinkles should merely indicate
where smiles have been.

MARK TWAIN

Let no man despise thy youth; but be thou
an example of the believers, in word, in
conversation, in charity, in spirit, in faith,
in purity .

1 Timothy 4:12

Age is a quality of mind.
If you have left your dreams behind,
If hope is cold,
If you no longer look ahead,
If your ambitions' fires are dead—
Then you are old.

But if from life you take the best,
And if in life you keep the jest,
If love you hold;
No matter how the years go by,
No matter how the birthdays fly—
You are not old.

AUTHOR UNKNOWN

CHALLENGE TO YOUTH

Build on, and make thy castles high and fair,
 Rising and reaching upward to the skies;
Listen to voices in the upper air,
 Nor lose thy simple faith in mysteries.

HENRY WADSWORTH LONGFELLOW
The Castle Builder

Youth! youth! how buoyant are thy hopes!
They turn,
Like marigolds, toward the sunny side.

JEAN INGELOW

To express one's feelings as the end draws near is too intimate a task. But I may mention one thought that comes to me . . . The riders in a race do not stop short when they reach the goal. There is a little finishing canter before coming to a standstill. There is a time to hear the kind voices of friends, and to say to oneself: "The work is done." But just as one says that, the answer comes: "The race is over, but the work is never done while the power to work remains." The canter that brings you to a standstill need not be only a coming to rest. It cannot be, while you still live. For to live is to function. That is all there is to living.

OLIVER WENDELL HOLMES

No Spring, no Summer beauty hath such grace,
As I have seen in an Autumnal face.

JOHN DONNE

Many blessings do the advancing years
bring with them.

HORACE

God gave us our memories so that we
might have roses in December.

SIR JAMES M. BARRIE

Lord God, burden my heart to reach out to the young persons start-
ing their adventure in life—and the old persons dreading the end of
the journey. Let me tell them the message of Your saving love. In
Jesus' name, amen.

—J. W. B.

Bible

All the good from the Saviour of the world is communicated through this Book. All the things desirable to man are contained in it.
—ABRAHAM LINCOLN

For hundreds of years during the Dark Ages the Bible was chained in monasteries, with only a few privileged monks allowed to read it. From out of the fifteenth century came a man who was used by God to liberate His Word. William Tyndale had a desire to translate the Bible from Latin into English so that the common people would be able to read it.

The works of Erasmus and Martin Luther had had a tremendous effect on Tyndale—they had awakened in him a longing to see everyone able to read the Word of God. When Tyndale tried to obtain permission to translate the New Testament, he was met with tremendous opposition from the hierarchy of the Church. Persecuted, he fled to Germany, and at Cologne in 1525, began translating the Gospels of Matthew and Mark. Three thousand copies were smuggled into England.

When Henry VIII heard of this he ordered that they be collected and burned immediately. Today only five or six copies are in existence. Tyndale finished translating the Bible and also wrote leaflets which told of the sole authority of the Scriptures in the Church. The king was furious when he heard this and ordered that he be found and imprisoned.

William Tyndale was betrayed by a spy, thrown into prison in Antwerp, Belgium, and remained there in dire conditions for two years. Finally, the king ordered his execution and the kindly Tyndale was brought before the dreaded stake to be burned. His heart still burdened for the common man, William Tyndale lifted his head and prayed—his last words being not for himself but for the king: "Lord, open the King of England's eyes!"

It was only a year after his death that God answered this prayer. That same king, Henry VIII, decreed that the Bible be published throughout England and allowed to be read by all the people.

—*J. W. B.*

To what greater inspiration and counsel can we turn than to the imperishable truth to be found in this treasure house, the Bible?

QUEEN ELIZABETH II

Thy word have I hid in mine heart, that I might not sin against thee.

Psalms 119:11

The Bible is like a telescope. If a man looks *through* his telescope, then he sees worlds beyond; but if he looks *at* his telescope, then he does not see anything but that. The Bible is a thing to be looked through, to see that which is beyond; but most people only look at it; and so they see only the dead letter.

PHILLIPS BROOKS

What you bring away from the Bible depends to some extent on what you carry to it.

OLIVER WENDELL HOLMES

Although one can derive inspiration from any portion of the Scripture, it is better to have an understanding of the general structure of the Bible to get the most out of it. The Old Testament is an account of a nation, Israel. Out of that nation came Jesus Christ, the Saviour of the world. The New Testament is an account of a Man, the Son of Man, the Saviour. God Himself became a man, so that we might know what He is like. His appearance on the earth was the central, most important event of history. The Old Testament gives the background for this event; the New Testament tells the story of its fulfillment. You will find a unity of thought and purpose which indicates that one mind inspired the writing of the whole.

BILLY GRAHAM
Day by Day With Billy Graham

If we would destroy the Christian religion,
we must first of all destroy man's belief in
the Bible.

FRANÇOIS VOLTAIRE

HOW TO GET THE MOST
OUT OF THE BIBLE

1. Come to the Word expectantly.
2. Come surrendering to the truths
   here revealed.
3. Come expecting to use the truths
   here revealed.
4. Come unhurriedly.
5. Come with a proper emphasis.
6. Come to it even if nothing apparently
   comes from your coming.

E. STANLEY JONES

THE ANVIL—GOD'S WORD

Last eve I passed beside a blacksmith's door,
   And heard the anvil ring the vesper chime;
Then looking in, I saw upon the floor
   Old hammers, worn with beating years of time.

"How many anvils have you had," said I,
   "To wear and batter all these hammers so?"
"Just one," said he, and then, with twinkling eye,
   "The anvil wears the hammers out, you know."

And so, thought I, the anvil of God's Word,
   For ages skeptic blows have beat upon;
Yet, though the noise of falling blows was heard,
   The anvil is unharmed—the hammers gone.

AUTHOR UNKNOWN

For the word of God is quick, and powerful, and sharper than any twoedged
sword . . . .

Hebrews 4:12

England has two books, one which she has
made and one which has made her:
Shakespeare and the Bible.

VICTOR HUGO

When Sir Walter Scott was dying he requested that his son-in-law
read to him. Upon being asked from which book, he replied, "Need you
ask? There is but one!"

Every soldier and sailor of the United
States should have a Testament . . . We
plead for a closer, wider and deeper study
of the Bible, so that our people may be in
fact, as well as in theory, "doers of the
Word and not hearers only."

THEODORE ROOSEVELT

The Bible is a book in comparison with
which all others are of minor importance,
and which in all my perplexities and dis-
tresses has never failed to give me light and
strength.

ROBERT E. LEE

The Bible is the book of all others to be read
at all ages and in all conditions of human
life . . . I speak as a man of the world to
men of the world, and I say to you, "Search
the Scriptures."

JOHN QUINCY ADAMS

The foundations of our society and our
government rest so much on the teachings
of the Bible that it would be difficult to
support them if faith in these teachings
should cease to be practically universal in
our country.

CALVIN COOLIDGE

I never knew all there was in the Bible until I spent those years in jail. I was constantly finding new treasures.

JOHN BUNYAN

For as the rain cometh down, and the snow from heaven, and returneth not thither, but watereth the earth, and maketh it bring forth and bud, that it may give seed to the sower, and bread to the eater: So shall my word be that goeth forth out of my mouth . . . .

Isaiah 55:10, 11

Unless we form the habit of going to the Bible in bright moments as well as in trouble, we cannot fully respond to its consolations because we lack equilibrium between light and darkness.

HELEN KELLER

Without the Bible the education of the child in the present state of society is impossible.

LEO TOLSTOY

We must remember who we are. The Bible tells us how God made man out of the dust of the earth. We are also told that our bodies will go back to dust. The Bible also tells us that God breathed into man "the breath of life; and man became a living soul." Don't let your dust make you forget your soul. Remember who you are.

CHARLES L. ALLEN

Lord God, the comfort and joy that I find each day as I read Your Word, gives me strength. Thank You for those who have gone before who gave their lives so that this privilege could be mine. In Jesus' name, amen.

—J. W. B.

God

Where there is faith, there is love;
Where there is love, there is peace;
Where there is peace, there is God;
And where there is God, there is no need.
                    —LEO TOLSTOY

In the nineteenth century in Czarist Russia, Count Leo Tolstoy was experiencing great dissatisfaction with his wealthy and aristocratic way of life. Converted to Christianity, he renounced his former background and developed a system of thought emphasizing faith, love, and peace. He found that God could meet the needs of his heart—needs that could never be met before, despite his wealth. In *My Conversion* Tolstoy wrote:

> Five years ago faith came to me. I believed in the doctrine of Jesus, and all my life was suddenly changed. I ceased to desire that which previously I had desired, and on the other hand, I took to desiring what I had never desired before. That which formerly used to appear good in my eyes appeared evil, and that which used to appear evil appeared good.

                    —J. W. B.

Once when I was going through a dark period I prayed and prayed, but the heavens seemed to be brass. I felt as though God had disappeared and that I was all alone with my trial and burden. It was a dark night for my soul. I wrote my mother about the experience, and will never forget her reply: "Son, there are many times when God withdraws to test your faith. He wants you to trust Him in the darkness. Now, Son, reach up by faith in the fog and you will find that His hand will be there." In tears I knelt by my bed and experienced an overwhelming sense of God's presence. Whether or not we sense and feel the presence of the Holy Spirit or one of the holy angels, by faith we are certain God will never leave us nor forsake us.

BILLY GRAHAM
Angels

There's a divinity that shapes our ends,
Rough-hew them how we will.
WILLIAM SHAKESPEARE
Hamlet

O Lord, thou knowest that which is best for us. Let this or that be done, as thou shalt please. Give what thou wilt, how much thou wilt, and when thou wilt.
THOMAS À KEMPIS

God does not communicate things to us so much as He just is Himself in us. We are the vessels, the containers, so that the first work after the new birth is to cultivate the habit of receptivity.

We become God's means of expressing Himself. If there is anything godly in us, it is God. Paul never criticized himself for his fears or negative reactions, because that was all he could give. We are the have-nots because God is the have. We don't condemn ourselves for being unwilling, because we are unwilling.

Only Christ has victory here. Redemption means that God has begun to will instead of you. Fear is natural, but it is sin to follow our fears; Christ is the real self in us.

Thus the Christian can say, "I may not know where I am, but I know where He is—in me." It is not that God *has* love or power or light; He *is* love and power and light. He does not share Himself, He just is Himself—in us.

NORMAN GRUBB
Rees Howells

The first of all beautiful things is the continual possession of God.

SAINT GREGORY OF NAZIANZUS

Life's greatest tragedy is to lose God and
not to miss him.

F. W. NORWOOD

It is only by forgetting yourself that you
draw near to God.

HENRY DAVID THOREAU

Be still, and know that I am God . . . .

Psalms 46:10

To be unknown of God is altogether too
much privacy.

THOMAS MERTON

> Sometimes a light surprises
>   The Christian while he sings;
> It is the Lord who rises
>   With healing in His wings.
>
> God moves in a mysterious way
>   His wonders to perform;
> He plants his footsteps on the sea
>   And rides upon the storm.

WILLIAM COWPER

To us also, through every star, through
every blade of grass, is not God made visible if we will open our minds and eyes?

THOMAS CARLYLE

Pray remember what I have recommended to you, which is, to think
often on God, by day, by night, in your business, and even in your
diversions. He is always near you and with you; leave Him not alone.
You would think it rude to leave a friend alone who came to visit you;

why, then, must God be neglected? Do not then forget Him, but think on Him often, adore Him continually, live and die with Him; this is the glorious employment of a Christian; in a word, this is our profession; if we do not know it we must learn it. I will endeavour to help you with my prayers. . . .

BROTHER LAWRENCE
The Practice of the Presence of God

Whoso draws nigh to God one step
    through doubtings dim,
God will advance a mile
    in blazing light to him.
AUTHOR UNKNOWN

No man has a right to lead such a life of contemplation as to forget in his own ease the service due to his neighbor; nor has any man a right to be so immersed in active life as to neglect the contemplation of God.
SAINT AUGUSTINE

Because he hath inclined his ear unto me, therefore will I call upon him as long as I live.

Psalms 116:2

My business is not to remake myself,
But make the absolute best of what God made.
ROBERT BROWNING
Bishop Blougram's Apology

God's will is in operation in our lives. There is a purpose for your life. I believe no person is an accident. Before you were born on the earth you existed in the mind of God. You can rebel against God, but ultimately you will be totally defeated. You can endure life as it comes and find no joy and peace in it. Or you can choose the will of God and make His will your will.

As Tennyson put it: "Our wills are ours, we know not how; our wills are ours, to make them thine."

How can I know the will of God for my life? Many will never know because God does not reveal Himself to triflers. No one can walk into His holy presence on hurrying feet. If you merely pray, "Lord, this is my will, I hope you will approve," you are wasting your breath. Only those who sincerely want God's will, and have faith enough in Him to dedicate themselves to His will, can ever know it. To pray, "Lord, show me Thy will, and if I like it I will accept it," is a futile prayer. You must accept it before you know it. Whether or not you can do that depends on what opinion you have of God.

CHARLES L. ALLEN

HIGH FLIGHT

Oh, I have slipped the surly bonds of earth,
And danced the skies on laughter-silvered wings;
Sunward I've climbed and joined the tumbling mirth
Of sun-split clouds—and done a hundred things
You have not dreamed of—wheeled and soared and swung
High in the sunlit silence. Hovering there,
I've chased the shouting wind along and flung
My eager craft through footless halls of air.
Up, up the long delirious, burning blue
I've topped the wind-swept heights with easy grace,
Where never lark, or even eagle, flew;
And, while with silent, lifting mind I've trod
The high untrespassed sanctity of space,
Put out my hand, and touched the face of God.

JOHN GILLESPIE MAGEE, JR.
(Written by a fighter pilot just before he was killed in World War II.)

As the marsh-hen secretly builds on the watery sod,
Behold I will build me a nest on the greatness of God;
I will fly in the greatness of God as the marsh-hen flies
In the freedom that fills all the space 'twixt the marsh and the skies:
By so many roots as the marsh-grass sends in the sod
I will heartily lay me a-hold on the greatness of God:
Oh, like to the greatness of God is the greatness within
The range of the marshes, the liberal marshes of Glynn.

SIDNEY LANIER
The Marshes of Glynn

Yet still there whispers the small voice within,
Heard through gain's silence, and o'er glory's din:
Whatever creed be taught or land be trod,
Man's conscience is the oracle of God.

LORD BYRON

Think through me, Thoughts of God,
    And let my own thoughts be
Lost like the sand-pools on the shore
    Of the eternal sea.

AMY CARMICHAEL
Toward Jerusalem

God—That unity of bests.

ELIZABETH BARRETT BROWNING

Take away anything I have, but do not take away the sweetness of
walking and talking with the King of Glory! It is good to let our thoughts
run away with us sometimes, concerning the greatness of our God and
His marvelous kindness to us. As we look back, what wonderful lead-
ings and providences we see; what encouragement we find for the future.

JOHN STAM

God is the presence, warm, all-enfolding,
    touching the drab world into brilliance, lifting
the sad heart into song, indescribable, beyond understanding,
        yet by a bird's note, a chord of music,
    a light at sunset, a sudden movement of rapt insight,
        a touch of love, making the whole universe
            a safe home for the soul.

AN EARLY CHRISTIAN

We talk about God's remembering us, as if it were a special effort. But if we could only know how truly we belong to God, it would be different. God's remembrance of us is the natural claiming of our life by Him as true part of His own.

PHILLIPS BROOKS

God be in my head,
  And in my understanding;

God be in my eyes,
  And in my looking;

God be in my mouth,
  And in my speaking;

God be in my heart,
  And in my thinking;

God be at my end,
  And at my departing.
Sarum Primer

When outward bound we boldly sail
  And leave the friendly shore,
Let not our hearts of courage fail
  Before the voyage is o'er.
We trust in Thee, whate'er befall;
Thy sea is great, our boats are small.

When homeward bound we gladly turn,
  O bring us safely there,
Where harbour-lights of friendship burn
  And peace is in the air.
We trust in Thee, whate'er befall;
Thy sea is great, our boats are small.

HENRY VAN DYKE
"Voyagers"

In a little while at five o'clock it is going to happen, and that is not so terrible . . . On the contrary, it is beautiful to be in God's strength. God has told us that He will not forsake us if only we pray to Him for support. I feel so strongly my nearness to God I am fully prepared to die . . . I have confessed all my sins to Him and have become very quiet. Therefore do not mourn but trust in God and pray for strength . . . Give me a firm handshake. God's will be done . . . Greet everybody for the four of us . . . We are courageous. Be the same. They can only take our bodies. Our souls are in God's hands . . . May God bless you all. Have no hate. I die without hatred. God rules everything.

(A letter by a Dutch patriot written just
prior to his execution by a Nazi firing squad)

Lord God, when I have experienced that restlessness that Saint Augustine spoke of, it seemed there was no answer to the myriad problems and longings of my soul. When I reach out to You, You fill this empty heart and bring a joy that is eternal. My joy relies completely on Your love and forgiveness. Thank You, my God and King! Amen.

—J. W. B.

Christmas

Christmas waves a magic wand over this world, and behold, everything is softer and more beautiful.

—NORMAN VINCENT PEALE

On Christmas Eve in Bethlehem in 1865, a young minister was deeply moved by a simple church service to commemorate Christ's birth. As he stood in the ancient building, which dated back to the fourth century, little did Phillips Brooks realize that just a few years later the memory of that scene would be used by him to write one of the most beautiful Christmas carols.

The Reverend Phillips Brooks, greatly loved minister of Holy Trinity Church in Boston, was a man who seemed larger than life. Not only was he an imposing figure physically—he stood six-feet-four-inches tall—but his magnanimous personality captivated all those who met him. One day after he had finished preaching, one of his parishioners turned to a friend and said, "I say, it makes you feel good just to look at him!"

In front of Holy Trinity Church there is a statue of Phillips Brooks. The sculptor, when he was first given the commission to carve the statue, studied all he could about this great man, hoping to find what made him so outstanding. After visiting Virginia, where Brooks had studied, his church in Philadelphia, and then back to Boston, he came to the conclusion that it was the love and power of Jesus Christ in Phillips Brooks's life. When the statue was unveiled the spectators saw not only Phillips Brooks, but standing behind him was the figure of Christ blessing him with His hands above the beloved minister's head.

One day during Phillips Brooks's ministry, he was asked by one of the children who attended the church school to write them a special Christmas song. Sitting down, he remembered the peaceful scene of Bethlehem, with the shepherd's fields close by, and in one evening he wrote the simple but meaningful verses that tell of God's incredible gift to mankind.

—*J. W. B.*

O little town of Bethlehem,
    How still we see thee lie!
Above thy deep and dreamless sleep
    The silent stars go by:
Yet in thy dark streets shineth
    The everlasting Light;
The hopes and fears of all the years
    Are met in thee to-night.

For Christ is born of Mary;
    And gathered all above,
While mortals sleep, the angels keep
    Their watch of wondering love.
O morning stars together
    Proclaim the holy birth!
And praises sing to God the King,
    And peace to men on earth.

How silently, how silently,
    The wondrous Gift is given!
So God imparts to human hearts
    The blessings of His heaven.
No ear may hear His coming,
    But in this world of sin,
Where meek souls will receive Him, still
    The dear Christ enters in.

O holy Child of Bethlehem,
    Descend to us, we pray;
Cast out our sin, and enter in,
    Be born in us to-day.
We hear the Christmas angels
    The great glad tidings tell;
O come to us, abide with us,
    Our Lord Emmanuel!

PHILLIPS BROOKS

It is in the Word that we receive and embrace him, and so where the Word of Christ dwells richly, there Christ dwells. If the Word be in us at home, then we abide in Christ, and he in us. The ground of our hope is Christ in the world, but the evidence of our hope is Christ in the heart.

MATTHEW HENRY

Now all this was done, that it might be fulfilled which was spoken of the Lord by the prophet, saying,

Behold, a virgin shall be with child, and shall bring forth a son, and they shall call his name Emmanuel, which being interpreted is, God with us.

Matthew 1:22, 23

There she was. The young woman with the radiant smile. She was leaning against one of the stalls, and the eyes in the happy face were closed. The man was at her side. And behind them, in the manger where the cows came for their food, was the Baby.

He was a tiny thing, wrapped tightly in a long linen band and sleeping as soundly as any newborn baby. Sleeping as though the world had not waited thousands of years for this moment. As soundly as though your life and my life and the life of everyone on earth were not wrapped up in His birth. As though from this moment on all the sin and sorrow of the world were not His problem.

Should you speak to His mother resting so quietly there? Should you ask her if you might touch the Baby—not to wake Him, but just to touch His hand?

What a moment that would have been! To have reached out your own hand and touched the Son of God!

RUTH BELL GRAHAM
Our Christmas Story

The most amazing thing about the Christmas story is its relevance. It is at home in every age and fits into every mood of life. It is not simply a lovely tale once told, but eternally contemporary. It is the voice crying out in every wilderness. It is as meaningful in our time as in that long-ago night when shepherds followed the light of the star to the manger of Bethlehem.

JOSEPH R. SIZOO

Are you willing—
    to stoop down and consider the needs and desires
        of little children;
    to remember the weakness and loneliness of people
        who are growing old;
    to stop asking how much your friends love you, and
    to ask yourself whether you love them enough;

to bear in mind the things that other people have to
   bear on their hearts;
to trim your lamp so that it will give more light and
   less smoke, and to carry it in front so that your
   shadow will fall behind you;
to make a grave for your ugly thoughts and a garden
   for your kindly feelings, with the gate open?
Are you willing to do these things for a day?
Then you are ready to keep Christmas!

HENRY VAN DYKE

MY GIFT

What can I give Him
Poor as I am?
If I were a shepherd,
I would give Him a lamb,
If I were a Wise Man,
I would do my part,—
But what I can I give Him,
Give my heart.

CHRISTINA G. ROSSETTI

Though Christ a thousand times
   In Bethlehem be born,
If He's not born in thee
   Thy soul is still forlorn.

From the German of
ANGELUS SILESIUS

Happy, happy Christmas, that can win us
back to the delusions of our childish days,
recall to the old man the pleasures of his
youth, and transport the traveler back to
his own fireside and quiet home!

CHARLES DICKENS

Before the paling of the stars,
   Before the winter morn,
Before the earliest cock-crow,
   Jesus Christ was born;

Born in a stable,
  Cradled in a manger;
In the world His hands had made,
  Born a stranger.

Priest and king lay fast asleep
  In Jerusalem;
Young and old lay fast asleep
  In crowded Bethlehem;
Saint and angel, ox and ass,
  Kept a watch together,
Before the Christmas day-break,
  In the winter weather.

Jesus on His mother's breast,
  In the stable cold,
Spotless Lamb of God was He,
  Shepherd of the fold:
Let us kneel with Mary maid,
  With Joseph bent and hoary,
With saint and angel, ox and ass,
  To hail the King of glory!
      CHRISTINA G. ROSSETTI

Therefore the Lord himself shall give you a sign; Behold, a virgin shall conceive, and bear a son, and shall call his name Immanuel . . . .

For unto us a child is born, unto us a son is given: and the government shall be upon his shoulder: and his name shall be called Wonderful, Counsellor, The mighty God, The everlasting Father, The Prince of Peace.

Isaiah 7:14; 9:6

FOR CHRISTMAS THE YEAR ROUND

"O come to my heart, Lord Jesus:
There is room in my heart for Thee."

Lord Jesus, we thank Thee for the spirit shed abroad in human hearts at Christmas. Even as we invited Thee at Christmas to be born again in our hearts, so wilt Thou now go with us throughout the days ahead, to be our Companion in all that we do. Wilt Thou help each one of us to keep Christmas alive in our hearts and in our homes, that it may continue to glow, to shed its warmth, to speak its message during all the bleak days of winter.

May we hold to that spirit, that we may be as gentle and as kindly today as we were on Christmas Eve, as generous tomorrow as we were on Christmas morning.

Then if—by Thy help—we should live through a whole week in that spirit, it may be we can go into another week, and thus be encouraged and gladdened by the discovery that Christmas can last the year round.

So give us joyful, cheerful hearts to the glory of Jesus Christ, our Lord, Amen.

PETER MARSHALL
The Prayers of Peter Marshall

WHEN JESUS SMILED

The cattle lay still in the darkened stalls;
    The smell of the hay was sweet;
Joseph kept watch through the long, still night
    At Mary's feet.

The windows were black and barred in the inn;
    The flocks on the hill were asleep;
Mary did look on the Babe by her side,
    And her thoughts were deep.

Timidly up to the manger crept two
    Young children, seeking to find
Shelter and rest. One boy was deaf;
    The other was blind.

The face of Mary was tender and calm
    As Joseph made room for them.
Nearer they came, till they knelt in the straw
    At her garment's hem.

Softly she crooned a lullaby low,
    And a great star lilied the night.
The singing was sweet to one little waif;
    To the other, the light.

Close to the heart of His mother lay,
    Like a blossom, the lovely Christ Child.
Softly He stirred and opened His eyes
    And slowly He smiled.

Suddenly then a wonderful thing,
    A beautiful thing, occurred:
The little blind boy cried, "Look, oh, look!"
    And the deaf boy heard.

MARY J. ELMENDORF

LET US KEEP CHRISTMAS

Whatever else be lost among the years,
Let us keep Christmas still a shining thing:
Whatever doubts assail us, or what fears,
Let us hold close one day, remembering
Its poignant meaning for the hearts of men.
Let us get back our childlike faith again.

GRACE NOLL CROWELL

CHRISTMAS

Once in royal David's city
    Stood a lowly cattle-shed,
Where a mother laid her baby
    In a manger for His bed.
Mary was that mother mild,
Jesus Christ her little child.

He came down to earth from heaven
    Who is God and Lord of all,
And His shelter was a stable,
    And His cradle was a stall.
With the poor and mean and lowly
Lived on earth our Saviour holy.

And our eyes at last shall see Him,
    Through His own redeeming love;
For that Child so dear and gentle
    Is our Lord in heaven above;
And He leads His children on
To the place where He is gone.

Not in that poor lowly stable,
  With the oxen standing by,
We shall see Him, but in heaven,
  Set at God's right hand on high,
When, like stars, His children crowned
All in white shall wait around.

CECIL F. ALEXANDER

Thank You, Heavenly Father, for the unspeakable gift of Your Son, Jesus Christ. Through it I see Your immeasurable love reaching down to all mankind. Cleanse my heart that it might be a sanctified gift for You. In Jesus' name, amen.

—J. W. B.

Jesus Christ

The fifteen-year-old boy, deep in thought, descended the steps of the church with his father. Isaac Watts had just attended another service and had listened to the congregation haltingly try to follow the singing of the Psalms. "The singing of God's praise is the part of worship nighest heaven and its performance among us is the worst," Isaac complained. He was immediately challenged by his father to write something better, and this was the beginning of a revolution in church music.

Isaac Watts has since become known as the "father of hymnology" and wrote a total of about six hundred hymns. In 1707 the first hymnbook was published containing his compositions, and among them was one that grew to be considered the finest hymn ever written. "When I Survey the Wondrous Cross" has been sung all over the world and the words still have the same momentous effect. Jesus Christ's great sacrifice, His suffering, and His love for all mankind are so simply conveyed, yet they strike deep within our hearts.

—*J. W. B.*

> When I survey the wondrous cross
>   On which the Prince of Glory died,
> My richest gain I count but loss,
>   And pour contempt on all my pride.
>
> Forbid it, Lord, that I should boast,
>   Save in the death of Christ, my God;
> All the vain things that charm me most,
>   I sacrifice them to His blood.

See, from His head, His hands, His feet
  Sorrow and love flow mingled down;
Did e'er such love and sorrow meet,
  Or thorns compose so rich a crown?

Were the whole realm of nature mine,
  That were a present far too small;
Love so amazing, so divine,
  Demands my soul, my life, my all. *Amen.*

ISAAC WATTS

There was a woman at a well, one day
Near a city of Samaria, in a land far away.
There she met a Stranger, who changed her life that day,
For He gave her living water—from
  The Truth, the Life, the Way.
She left her waterpot, there by the well,
Ran into the city—*for she must tell*
  That she had met the Messiah at the well!

DALE EVANS ROGERS
The Woman at the Well

The storm was raging. The sea was beating against the rocks in huge, dashing waves. The lightning was flashing, the thunder was roaring, the wind was blowing; but the little bird was sound asleep in the crevice of the rock, its head tucked serenely under its wing. That is peace: to be able to sleep in the storm!

In Christ we are relaxed and at peace in the midst of the confusions, bewilderments and perplexities of this life. The storm rages, but our hearts are at rest. We have found peace—at last!

BILLY GRAHAM
Peace With God

O Christ who holds the open gate,
O Christ who drives the furrow straight . . .
Lo, all my heart's field red and torn,
And Thou wilt bring the young green corn,
The young green corn divinely springing;
The young green corn forever singing;
And when the field is fresh and fair

Thy blessed feet shall glitter there
And we will walk the weeded field,
And tell the golden harvest's yield,
The corn that makes the holy bread
By which the soul of man is fed,
The holy bread, the food unpriced,
Thy everlasting mercy, Christ.

JOHN MASEFIELD

I have loved to hear my Lord spoken of,
and wherever I have seen the print of His
shoe in the earth, there have I coveted to
put mine also.

JOHN BUNYAN

FAITH

So through the clouds of Calvary—there shines
His face, and I believe that evil dies,
And good lives on, loves on, and conquers all—
All war must end in peace. These clouds are lies.
They cannot last. The blue sky is the truth.
For God is Love. Such is my faith, and such
My reasons for it, and I find them strong
Enough. And you? You want to argue? Well,
I can't. It is a choice. I choose the Christ.

G. A. STUDDERT-KENNEDY

I thank God for the honesty and virility of
Jesus' religion which makes us face the
facts and calls us to take a man's part in the
real battle of life.

HENRY VAN DYKE

The men who followed Him were unique
in their generation. They turned the world
upside down because their hearts had been
turned right side up. The world has never
been the same.

BILLY GRAHAM

They will kill me if they please, but they
will never, never tear the living Christ from
my heart.
                                    SAVONAROLA

Jesus, whose name is not so much written
as ploughed in the history of this world.
                              RALPH WALDO EMERSON

I know that Christ is interested in every detail of my daily life and of
        yours.
And why not?
If He has numbered the hairs of our heads . . .
        if He notes the sparrow's fall . . .
shall He not care about what we do every day and how we do it?

Most of us simply refuse to believe how practical God is.

He is ready to tell us what to say in an important conversation.
He is ready to help us make the right decision in a difficult choice.
He is ready to guide the hand of the surgeon,
        and the scissors of the housewife.
He is ready to give new strength to the tired servant standing over the
kitchen sink.
                              PETER MARSHALL
                              "The Tap on the Shoulder"

Thanks be to Thee, my Lord Jesus Christ,
For all the benefits which Thou hast given me.
But all the pains and insults which thou hast borne for me.
O, most merciful Redeemer, Friend and Brother,
May I know Thee more clearly,
Love Thee more dearly,
And follow Thee more nearly.
                                    RICHARD
                                    Bishop of Chichester.

The Lord has turned all our sunsets
into sunrise.
                        CLEMENT OF ALEXANDRIA

. . . Christ in you, the hope of glory.
                        Colossians 1:27

The moment I awaked, "Jesus, Master,"
was in my heart and in my mouth; and I
found all my strength lay in keeping my
eye fixed upon him, and my soul waiting
on him continually.

JOHN WESLEY's *Journal*
May 25, 1738

Alexander, Caesar, Charlemagne, and
myself founded empires; but on what
foundation did we rest the creations of our
genius? Upon force. Jesus Christ founded
an empire upon love; and at this hour millions of men would die for Him.

NAPOLEON BONAPARTE

He comes to us as one unknown, without a name, as of old by the
lakeside he came to those men who knew him not. He speaks to us the
same word, "Follow thou me," and sets us to the tasks which he has to
fulfill for our time. He commands. And to those who obey, whether they
be wise or simple, he will reveal himself in the toils, the conflicts, the
suffering which they shall pass through in his fellowship, and as an
ineffable mystery, they shall learn in their own experience who he is.

ALBERT SCHWEITZER

Son of man, whenever I doubt of life I think
of thee. Thou never growest old to me. Last
century is old. Last year is obsolete fashion, but thou art not obsolete. Thou art
abreast of all the centuries, and I have
never come up to thee, modern as I am.

GEORGE MATHESON

No one else holds or has held the place in
the heart of the world which Jesus holds.
Other gods have been as devoutly wor-
shiped; no other man has been so devoutly
loved.

JOHN KNOX

In Jesus I see the picture of the kind of man
I know I ought to be.

WILLIAM ADAMS BROWN

To those who fall, how kind thou art;
How good to those who seek;
But what to those who find? Ah, this
Nor tongue nor pen can show:
The love of Jesus, what it is,
None but his loved ones know.

BERNARD OF CLAIRVAUX

To be in Christ, is to live in His ideas, character, spirit, as the atmosphere of being. Men everywhere are living in the ideas and characters
of others. He who lives in the spirit of Raphael, becomes a painter; he
who lives in the spirit of Milton, becomes a poet; he who lives in the
spirit of Bacon, becomes a philosopher; he who lives in the spirit of
Caesar, becomes a warrior; he who lives in the spirit of Christ, becomes
a man.

AUTHOR UNKNOWN

Jesus is God spelling himself out in language that man can understand.

S. D. GORDON

Above all the grace and the gifts that Christ
gives to his beloved is that of overcoming
self.

SAINT FRANCIS OF ASSISI

By a Carpenter mankind was made, and
only by that Carpenter can mankind be remade.

ERASMUS

Jesus hath many lovers of His kingdom, but few bearers of His cross. All are disposed to rejoice with Him, but few suffer sorrow for His sake. Many follow Him to the breaking of the bread, but few to the drinking of His bitter cup.

THOMAS À KEMPIS

Shall I tell you what supported me through all these years of exile among a people whose language I could not understand, and whose attitude toward me was always uncertain and often hostile? It was this, "Lo, I am with you alway even unto the end of the world."

DAVID LIVINGSTONE

I, if I be lifted up from the earth, will draw all men unto me.

This he said, signifying what death he should die.

John 12:32, 33

They borrowed a bed to lay his head
    When Christ the Lord came down;
They borrowed the ass in the mountain pass
    For him to ride to town;
But the crown that he wore and the cross that he bore
Were his own—
The cross was his own.

AUTHOR UNKNOWN

More than nineteen hundred years have passed . . .
The Cross itself has long since crumbled into dust.
Yet, it stands again when we choose our own Calvary and crucify Him all over again, with every sin of commission and omission.

> Every wrong attitude . . .
>   every bad disposition . . .
> every unkind word . . .
>   every impure imagination . . .
>   every ignoble desire . . .
>   every unworthy ambition . . .

Yes, Calvary still stands, and the crowd at the top of the hill.

Were you there when they crucified my Lord?
I was . . . Were you?

PETER MARSHALL
Mr. Jones, Meet the Master

WHEN JESUS COMES, THE SHADOWS DEPART.
Inscription on Scottish castle wall

Lord Jesus, Saviour and Lord, I worship and praise You! Your sacrifice for me overwhelms my heart when I think of all You suffered. But, Lord, in spite of the unworthiness of my life, You love me. How I want others to know of the love You are waiting to give them too. Amen.

—J. W. B.

Easter

And He departed from our sight that we
might return to our heart, and there find Him.
For He departed, and behold, He is here.
—SAINT AUGUSTINE

I know that Christ is alive,
        and personal
    and real, and closer than we think.
I have met Him.
I have felt His presence.
            "The Tap on the Shoulder"

These are the words of a Scottish immigrant who became Chaplain to the United States Senate. Peter Marshall never lost his simple faith in the living Christ from the day he was deeply touched by a missionary appeal in a little church in Scotland. God was to lead him to America where he would marry the greatly loved writer Catherine Marshall, and together they would serve Christ in a dynamic and far-reaching ministry.

Peter Marshall attended seminary and then pastored a Presbyterian church in Georgia. Later he was called to Washington, D.C., and ministered at the National Presbyterian Church. His sermons were like word pictures painted by a great love and desire to show the living Christ to all who sat and listened to him. On January 4, 1947, he was made Chaplain to the Senate by the Republican majority—two years later he was reappointed by the Democratic majority. His life showed his rugged, dynamic faith. He spoke with courage, compassion, and always with hope.

When Peter Marshall died suddenly of a heart attack at the age of forty-six, it seemed that God had cut off a ministry that the world needed desperately. But

God was to use Peter's wife, Catherine, to carry on his work, and with courage and inspiration she went through his notes and published the sermons which had blessed his congregations. In turn they blessed far greater numbers of people than Peter Marshall had ever dreamed they could, and still today they go on inspiring and encouraging all those who read them.

After her husband's early death, Catherine Marshall published these words in *A Man Called Peter:*

> But I believe it will be like this—Jesus will come over and lay his hand across my shoulders and say to God, "Yes, all these things are true, but I'm here to cover up for Peter. He is sorry for all his sins, and by a transaction made between us, I am now solely responsible for them."

In this excerpt from one of Peter Marshall's Easter sermons we are reminded again of the hope and joy of Christ's Resurrection:

> The glorious fact that the empty tomb proclaims to us is that life for us does not stop when death comes.
>
> Death is not a wall, but a door.
>
> And eternal life which may be ours now, by faith in Christ, is not interrupted when the soul leaves the body,
>   for we live on . . . and on.
>
> *There is no death to those who have entered into fellowship with Him who emerged from the tomb.*
>
> Because the Resurrection is true, it is the most significant thing in our world today. Bringing the Resurrected Christ into our lives, individual and national, is the only hope we have for making a better world.
>
> "Because I live, ye shall live also."
>
> That is the message of Easter.

—J. W. B.

In the end of the sabbath, as it began to dawn toward the first day of the week, came Mary Magdalene and the other Mary to see the sepulchre.

And, behold . . . the angel of the Lord descended from heaven, and came and rolled back the stone from the door . . . .

And the angel . . . said unto the women, Fear not ye: for I know that ye seek Jesus, which was crucified.

He is not here: for he is risen, as he said. Come, see the place where the Lord lay.

And go quickly, and tell his disciples that he is risen from the dead; and, behold, he goeth before you into Galilee; there shall ye see him . . . .

Matthew 28:1, 2, 5–7

We thank Thee for the beauty of this day, for the glorious message that all nature proclaims: The Easter lilies with their waxen throats eloquently singing the good news; the birds, so early this morning impatient to begin their song; every flowering tree, shrub, and flaming bush, a living proclamation from Thee. O open our hearts that we may hear it, too!

Lead us, we pray Thee, to the grave that is empty, into the Garden of the Resurrection where we may meet our risen Lord. May we never again live as if Thou were dead!

In Thy presence restore our faith, our hope, our joy. Grant to our spirits refreshment, rest, and peace. Maintain within our hearts an unruffled calm, an unbroken serenity that no storms of life shall ever be able to take from us.

From this moment, O living Christ, we ask Thee to go with us wherever we go; be our companion in all that we do. And for this greatest of all gifts, we offer Thee our sacrifices of thanksgiving. *Amen.*

PETER MARSHALL
The Prayers of Peter Marshall

> Christ the Lord is risen today,
> > Alleluia!
> Sons of men and angels say
> > Alleluia!
> Raise your joys and triumphs high;
> > Alleluia!
> Sing, ye heavens, and earth reply,
> > Alleluia!

Lives again our glorious King;
    Alleluia!
Where, O death, is now thy sting?
    Alleluia!
Dying once, He all doth save;
    Alleluia!
Where thy victory, O grave?
    Alleluia!

Love's redeeming work is done,
    Alleluia!
Fought the fight, the battle won;
    Alleluia!
Death in vain forbids Him rise;
    Alleluia!
Christ has opened Paradise.
    Alleluia!

Soar we now where Christ has led;
    Alleluia!
Following our exalted Head;
    Alleluia!
Made like Him, like Him we rise;
    Alleluia!
Ours the cross, the grave, the skies.
    Alleluia!

CHARLES WESLEY

Our Lord has written the promise of the resurrection, not in books alone, but in every leaf in springtime.

MARTIN LUTHER

Tomb, thou shalt not hold Him longer;
Death is strong, but Life is stronger;
Stronger than the dark, the light;
Stronger than the wrong, the right;
Faith and Hope triumphant say,
Christ will rise on Easter Day.

PHILLIPS BROOKS

Then came the end. He was accused of stirring up the people. He was placed on trial. He was charged with blasphemy. Did He not claim to be the promised Messiah? At least, did He not allow people to get the impression that He was the Son of God? In His public trial He was challenged to deny His deity, to withdraw His blasphemous statements, and clear up the confused minds of the simple people who believed Him to be God visiting earth in human form.

But He could not tell a lie, so He remained silent. The verdict was predictable: death by crucifixion! A crowd gathered to see how a possibility thinker dies. How did He die? He died seeing and seizing the possibilities of the moment! He practiced what He had preached all His life! He turned the hell into a heaven.

For here was His chance to save the soul of a lost thief who was being crucified beside Him.

". . . *today you will be with me in Paradise*" (Luke 23:43).

Here was His chance to teach the world how forgiving God can be!

"*Father, forgive them; for they know not what they do*" (Luke 23:34).

This was a spectacular opportunity to dramatically teach all men of all ages to come that death can be a grand reunion with God!

So His last spoken words were loaded with great expectations. "*Father, into thy hands I commit my spirit*" (Luke 23:46)!

There was a final gasp—and He was gone. The Roman commander in charge of the execution turned away—converted on the spot, he was overheard saying, "*Certainly this man was innocent*" (Luke 23:47)!

The body was taken down and sealed in a tomb. Then it happened! Easter! He was resurrected. He came back to life again.

Why do we believe this fantastic tale? Because of the incredible change in His followers. They saw Him alive again. Where they were cowards, they became fearless proclaimers in the city streets—in daylight! Where they were impossibility thinkers—they became possibility thinkers!

ROBERT H. SCHULLER
*The Greatest Possibility
Thinker That Ever Lived*

BECAUSE HE LIVES

Because He lives I can face tomorrow,
Because He lives all fear is gone.
Because I know He holds the future,
And life is worth the living,
Just because He lives.

WILLIAM AND GLORIA GAITHER

"IF I SHOULD WAKE BEFORE I DIE"

The father knelt down beside his little boy's bed. It was time for prayers, hugs of affirmation and tender tucking in.

The little boy began his childhood prayer repeated so many times before . . .

Now I lay me down to sleep;
I pray the Lord my soul to keep.
If I should die before I wake,
I pray the Lord, my soul to take.

This night the words got mixed up and unknown to the child he spoke words of the greatest wisdom he would ever come to know . . . .

He prayed:

If I should wake before I die . . . .

Then he stopped in embarrassed apologies:

"Oh, Daddy, I got all mixed up."

Wisely, his Daddy responded with tender care . . .

"Not at all, son, that's the first time that prayer was properly prayed . . . My deepest longing for you is that you may wake up before you die."

The child drifted into childhood sleep, but the father turned the prophetic words about in his mind.

"If I should wake before I die . . . ."

"That's it!" he exclaimed. "That's the promise of the Good News of Easter. This is the time to come alive and live forever! That's the hope of Easter."

LLOYD JOHN OGILVIE

. . . because I live, ye shall live also.
John 14:19

EASTER

Sing, soul of mine, this day of days,
  The Lord is risen.
Toward the sun-rising set thy face,
  The Lord is risen.
Behold He giveth strength and grace;
For darkness, light; for mourning, praise;
For sin, his holiness; for conflict, peace.

Arise, O soul, this Easter Day!
Forget the tomb of yesterday,
For thou from bondage art set free;
Thou sharest in His victory
And life eternal is for thee,
Because the Lord is risen.

AUTHOR UNKNOWN

There are people
  waiting
    waiting
      waiting
for man?
No.
Man has exhausted their patience.
What does man offer but broken plays
and unfinished puzzles?
They are waiting for God.
They are waiting for the angel
to roll away
the stone.

SHERWOOD E. WIRT
Decision magazine

O Living Christ, my heart and soul praise You for the light that pervades the deepest gloom and transforms my life with Your love!
—*J. W. B.*

Immortality

It is not darkness you are going to, for God is
Light. It is not lonely, for Christ is with you. It
is not an unknown country, for Christ is there.
                                        —CHARLES KINGSLEY

I cannot possibly use the word *happy* without meaning something beyond
this present life." These were the words of Christina G. Rossetti, England's
leading poetess of the Victorian era. Her faith in a life after death dominated her
poetry and everyday living.

Christina was born in England in 1830. She was taught entirely at home and
had great problems with her reading, although she excelled in writing.
Everyone thought her a pretty child, with hazel eyes and light brown hair, and
her high-spirited, playful ways made her a favorite of the visitors to the Rossetti
household. Her father was a political refugee from Italy, and the house was
often filled with other refugees—many of them painters and writers. This had
an influence on the lives of all the Rossetti children. Christina's brother Dante
became a highly successful poet and painter and she often served as a model for
him. Her sister wrote verse until she entered a convent.

Christina Rossetti's tender, sincere, and affectionate life was completely regu-
lated by her devout, childlike trust in God. She showed absolute faith at a time
when there was great skepticism—"My faith is faith" would be her response to
any argument questioning her belief. Twice she refused to marry because of her
religious convictions—her second suitor Charles Cayley seemed to be completely uncertain of his belief in anything. She loved him until the day she died,
and many of her poems refer to her love for him.

Christina Rossetti suffered greatly before she died, but her poetry shows the
triumph over suffering because she saw beyond her transitory life to one that
she would live with her beloved Lord—eternally. Her love for Him is shown in
this poem:

THE LOWEST PLACE

Give me the lowest place, not that I dare
  Ask for that lowest place, but Thou hast died
That I might live and share
  Thy glory by Thy side.

Give me the lowest place; or if for me
  That lowest place too high, make one more low
Where I may sit and see
  My God and love Thee so.

The last four lines are inscribed on her gravestone at Highgate, England, and seem to epitomize this gentle, loving soul's life.

                                                 —*J. W. B.*

SONG

When I am dead, my dearest,
  Sing no sad songs for me;
Plant thou no roses at my head,
  Nor shady cypress-tree;
Be the green grass above me
  With showers and dewdrops wet;
And if thou wilt, remember,
  And if thou wilt, forget.

I shall not see the shadows,
  I shall not feel the rain;
I shall not hear the nightingale
  Sing on, as if in pain;
And dreaming through the twilight
  That doth not rise nor set,
Haply I may remember,
  And haply may forget.

                       CHRISTINA G. ROSSETTI

Jesus said unto her, I am the resurrection, and the life: he that believeth in me, though he were dead, yet shall he live: And whosoever liveth and believeth in me shall never die . . . .

                       John 11:25, 26

Our Creator would never have made such lovely days and have given us the deep hearts to enjoy them, above and beyond all thought, unless we were meant to be immortal.

NATHANIEL HAWTHORNE

We only see a little of the ocean,
A few miles distance from the rocky shore;
But oh! out there beyond—beyond the eyes' horizon
  There's more—there's more.

We only see a little of God's loving,
A few rich treasures from His mighty store;
But oh! out there beyond—beyond our life's horizon
  There's more—there's more.

AUTHOR UNKNOWN

The nearer I approach the end, the plainer I hear around me the immortal symphonies of the world to come. For half a century I have been writing my thoughts in prose and verse; but I feel that I have not said one-thousandth part of what is in me. When I have gone down to the grave I shall have ended my day's work; but another day will begin the next morning. Life closes in the twilight but opens with the dawn.

VICTOR HUGO

The glory of the star, the glory of the sun—we must not lose either in the other. We must not be so full of the hope of heaven that we cannot do our work on the earth; we must not be so lost in the work of the earth that we shall not be inspired by the hope of heaven.

PHILLIPS BROOKS

Each departed friend is a magnet that attracts us to the next world.

JEAN PAUL RICHTER

What is our death but a night's sleep? For
as through sleep all weariness and faint-
ness pass away and cease, and the powers
of the spirit come back again, so that in the
morning we arise fresh and strong and joyous; so at the Last Day we shall rise again
as if we had only slept a night, and shall be
fresh and strong.

MARTIN LUTHER

Here on this earth we are gathered together in families. Our loved
ones become inexpressibly precious to us. We live in intimate associa-
tions. One gets so close to mother and father, wife or husband, sons and
daughters, that they literally become a part of one's life. Then comes a
day when a strange change comes over one we love.

He is transformed before our very eyes. The light of life goes out of
him. He cannot speak to us nor we to him. He is gone and we are left
stunned and heartbroken. An emptiness and loneliness comes into our
hearts. We broken-heartedly say, "That one whom I loved is dead." It is
such a cold, hopeless thing to realize.

Then, out of the very depths of our despair, like the melody of music
coming from a mighty organ, like the refreshing sound of rippling waters, comes that marvelous declaration of our Lord. "I am the resurrection, and the life: he that believeth in me, though he were dead, yet shall
he live: and whosoever liveth and believeth in me shall never die."

Then we know! We *know* we have not lost our loved ones who have
died. We have been separated, and so long as we live there will be an
empty place left in our hearts. To some extent, the loneliness will always
be there. But when we really know that one is not forever lost, it does
take away the sorrow. There is a vast difference between precious
memories, loneliness, the pain of separation, on the one hand, and a
sorrow that ruins and blights our lives, on the other hand.

CHARLES L. ALLEN

For as in Adam all die, even so in Christ
shall all be made alive.

1 Corinthians 15:22

> Music, when soft voices die,
> Vibrates in the memory—
> Odors, when sweet violets sicken,
> Live within the sense they quicken.
> Rose leaves, when the rose is dead,
> Are heap'd for the beloved's bed;
> And so thy thoughts, when thou art gone,
> Love itself shall slumber on.
>
> PERCY BYSSHE SHELLEY

Ever since the world began we have been experiencing life and death. The dying part of living has been with us in the past and it will remain with us in the future until God Himself calls an end to this existence as we know it.

My soul can accept the realities of death and dying, the sorrows of grieving, and the living I must continue to do, if I am willing to listen to God's song.

The early Christians heard the mourning song of God and as they were being led to their horrendous deaths in the Roman arena, they picked up mourning song's tune and we are told "went to their death— singing." It is not possible to be scared to death and still sing. The vocal cords restrict themselves into hard, rigid, tautly pulled ropes that will not work. So those martyred Christians had to have the song of God's confidence and joy really bursting within them in order to have filled the Coliseum with the sound of their music.

When I read, "Tears of joy shall stream down their faces, and I will lead them home with great care" (Jeremiah 31:9), I can, in my mind's eye, see not only those early Christians, but all the precious children of God we have lost; and, as if they are being filmed for a great movie spectacular, they stand together, all on a supersized screen. They stand as a gigantic host of people in front of me and the stereophonic music pours out of hundreds of speakers over my soul. Beautifully, as I listen and watch, I see God leading them *home*—with "great care."

Over the visual picture and above the sound of the triumphant music, I hear the narrator. He reads from a script written by Jeremiah and his resonant words ring deep and clear:

They shall come home and sing songs of
joy upon the hills of Zion, and shall be
radiant over the goodness of the Lord . . .
Their life shall be like a watered garden,
and all their sorrows shall be gone.

Jeremiah 31:12 (Living Bible)

JOYCE LANDORF
Mourning Song

What a man believes about immortality
will color his thinking in every area of life.

JOHN SUTHERLAND BONNELL

HOME

Think of stepping on shore and finding it Heaven!
Of taking hold of a hand and finding it God's!
Of breathing a new air and finding it celestial air!
Of feeling invigorated and finding it immortality!
Of passing from storm and stress to a perfect calm!
Of waking and finding it Home!

AUTHOR UNKNOWN

All mankind is of one Author, and is one volume; when one man dies,
one chapter is not torn out of the book, but translated into a better
language; and every chapter must be so translated; God employs several
translators; some pieces are translated by age, some by sickness, some
by war, some by justice; but God's hand is in every translation; and his
hand shall bind up all our scattered leaves again, for that library where
every book shall lie open to one another.

JOHN DONNE

I asked for Peace—
    My sins arose,
    And bound me close,
I could not find release.

I asked for Truth—
    My doubts came in,
    And with their din
They wearied all my youth.

I asked for Love—
    My lovers failed,
    And griefs assailed
Around, beneath, above.

I asked for Thee—
    And Thou didst come
    To take me home
Within Thy Heart to be.
                    DIGBY M. DOLBEN

THE CHARIOT

Because I could not stop for Death,
He kindly stopped for me;
The carriage held but just ourselves
And Immortality.

We slowly drove, he knew no haste,
And I had put away
My labor, and my leisure, too,
For his civility.

We passed the school where children played,
Their lessons scarcely done;
We passed the fields of gazing grain,
We passed the setting sun.

We paused before a house that seemed
A swelling on the ground;
The roof was scarcely visible,
The cornice but a mound.

Since then 'tis centuries; but each
Feels shorter than the day
I first surmised the horses' heads
Were toward eternity.
                    EMILY DICKINSON

How well he fell asleep!
Like some proud river, widening toward the sea;
Calmly and grandly, silently and deep,
    Life joined eternity.
                    SAMUEL TAYLOR COLERIDGE

The truest end of life is to know that life
never ends . . . Death is no more than a
turning of us over from time to eternity.
                                    WILLIAM PENN

Life is a voyage that's homeward bound.
                                    HERMAN MELVILLE

CROSSING THE BAR

Sunset and evening star,
  And one clear call for me!
And may there be no moaning of the bar,
  When I put out to sea,

But such a tide as moving seems asleep,
  Too full for sound and foam,
When that which drew from out the boundless deep
  Turns again home.

Twilight and evening bell,
  And after that the dark!
And may there be no sadness of farewell,
  When I embark;

For tho' from out our bourne of Time and Place
  The flood may bear me far,
I hope to see my Pilot face to face
  When I have crost the bar.
                                    ALFRED LORD TENNYSON

Let not your heart be troubled: ye believe
in God, believe also in me. In my Father's
house are many mansions: if it were not so,
I would have told you. I go to prepare a
place for you.
                                    John 14:1, 2

That day which you fear as being the end of
all things is the birthday of your eternity.
                                    SENECA

PRAYER BEFORE EXECUTION

O merciful Father, my hope is in Thee!
O Gracious Redeemer, deliver Thou me!
My bondage bemoaning, with sorrowful groaning,
    I long to be free:
Lamenting, relenting, and humbly repenting,
O Jesu, my Saviour, I languish for Thee!

MARY, QUEEN OF SCOTS

Pilot, how far from home?—
    Not far, not far tonight,
    A flight of spray, a sea-bird's flight,
A flight of tossing foam,
    And then the lights of home!

.   .   .   .

Pilot, how far from home?—
    The great stars pass away
    Before Him as a flight of spray,
Moons as a flight of foam!
    I see the lights of home.

ALFRED NOYES
"Harbor Lights"

Depart then without fear of this world even
as you came into it. The same way you
came from death to life, return from life to
death. Yield your torch to others as in a
race. Your death is but a piece of the
world's order, but a parcel of the world's
life.

MICHEL DE MONTAIGNE

Death is not death if it kills no part of us, save that which hindered
    us from perfect life.
Death is not death if it raises us in a moment from darkness into
    light, from weakness into strength, from sinfulness into holiness.
Death is not death if it brings us nearer to Christ, who is the fount of
    life.

Death is not death if it perfects our faith by sight and lets us behold Him in whom we have believed.

Death is not death if it gives us to those whom we have loved and lost, for whom we have lived, for whom we long to live again.

Death is not death if it rids us of doubt and fear, of chance and change, of space and time, and all which space and time bring forth and then destroy.

Death is not death, for Christ has conquered Death for Himself and for those who trust in Him.

CHARLES KINGSLEY

I thank You, Lord Jesus, for the peace of knowing that when my time comes to cross into eternity, You will be there to shepherd me. On wings of joy, I will reach out and take Your hand and look into Your blessed face! Amen.

—J. W. B.

Author Index

Topic Index